PRAISE FOR *SOCIALISM*

"For those horrified by the growth of the right and deflated by the ineptitude of the US liberal establishment, writer Danny Katch shows that there is a different way. *Socialism . . . Seriously* is a refreshing embrace of socialism as an alternative to the greed, inequality, racism, and xenophobia of the capitalist world we are living in. Katch dives straight into the questions about its possibility and potential with serious historical insights, a devout sense of humor, and a refreshing commitment to social change. The right book at the right time!" —**KEEANGA-YAMAHTTA TAYLOR**, author of *From #BlackLivesMatter to Black Liberation*

"Marx once said, 'Outside of a dog, a book is a man's best friend. Inside of a dog, it's too dark to read.' If you, like me, are outside of a dog, then you'll find the spirit of Groucho's words embodied in this brilliant, hilarious, and necessary companion to understanding our hyper-capitalist age. Give this to your grandma, your mailman, to everyone except your boss—it's the most fun and accessible introduction to socialist ideas I've ever read." —**ANAND GOPAL**, author of *No Good Men Among the Living*

"Reading *Socialism . . . Seriously* is like having your sometimes charming, sometimes quirky uncle sit next to you at dinner. He regales you with examples of today's rising rebellions along with fascinating history and critical analysis, occasionally interrupting himself with self-deprecating personal stories and cultural references to movies and moments you had tried to forget. He pokes and prods you every time he catches you doomscrolling on your phone, and somehow by the end of the night, he has convinced you that all is not lost, that humanity is something to believe in, and that a socialist world might even be possible. Read *Socialism . . . Seriously,* then pass it on to a friend. It's the perfect gateway drug to becoming the full-throttled socialist organizer that you've been waiting for." —**HADAS THIER**, author of *A People's Guide to Capitalism*

"With wit and wisdom, Danny Katch clarifies our political moment, but never falls into its thrall: we're in a five-alarm shit-storm of trouble, true, but Katch maintains that Love and Imagination, potentially the most powerful weapons in the arsenal of the oppressed and the exploited, are still within reach and entirely available. The promise of a more lovely world is worth our best energies and our sustained commitment—Danny Katch shows us that socialism is for lovers, not losers." —**BILL AYERS**, author of *Demand the Impossible!*

"Capitalism was a system built to be skewered. But to do it right, you need the political chops and you need to know how to make the jokes. Danny Katch checks every box, and his *Socialism . . . Seriously* is a necessary book, particularly for people who think politics are dry and especially for those who want to dismantle the system but don't know what to build in its place." —**DAVE ZIRIN**, author of *The Kaepernick Effect*

"I've been waiting for someone to write this book—a lighthearted, easy read that packs an intro course on socialism into a short volume. With jokes that made me laugh out loud, and a lot of heart. Socialism is for lovers. Indeed." —**SARAH JAFFE**, author of *Work Won't Love You Back*

"Danny Katch brings the socialist vision to life." —**BHASKAR SUNKARA**, editor of *Jacobin*

SOCIALISM . . . SERIOUSLY

A BRIEF GUIDE TO SURVIVING THE TWENTY-FIRST CENTURY

Revised and updated edition

DANNY KATCH

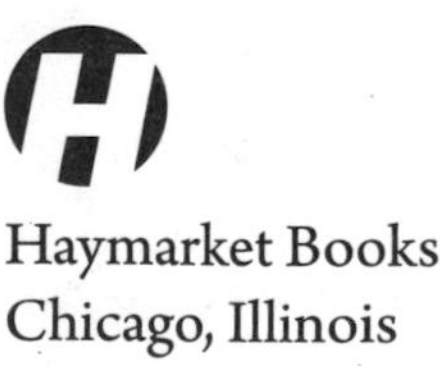

Haymarket Books
Chicago, Illinois

Published in 2023 by
Haymarket Books
P.O. Box 180165
Chicago, IL 60618
773-583-7884
www.haymarketbooks.org
info@haymarketbooks.org

ISBN: 978-1-64259-832-2

Distributed to the trade in the US through Consortium Book Sales and Distribution (www.cbsd.com) and internationally through Ingram Publisher Services International (www.ingramcontent.com).

This book was published with the generous support of Lannan Foundation and Wallace Action Fund.

Special discounts are available for bulk purchases by organizations and institutions. Please email info@haymarketbooks.org for more information.

Cover design by Steve Leard.
Illustrations by Sanaa Khan.

Printed in Canada by union labor.

Library of Congress Cataloging-in-Publication data is available.

10 9 8 7 6 5 4 3 2 1

Contents

Introduction

I wrote the first version of this book in early 2014, when TikTok was a Ke$ha song, Donald Trump was a joke, and Alexandria Ocasio-Cortez was a bartender. #BlackLivesMatter was a hashtag but not a movement, #MeToo was neither, and Mark Zuckerberg was a boy genius bringing the world together through his social network. We talked about climate change in the future tense and fascism in the past, and only wore masks at Halloween parties, bank robberies, and lucha libre wrestling matches.

For our purposes here, the most important change is that socialism was reborn, right here in the US of A, during Bernie Sanders's historic 2016 presidential campaign. Sadly, however, socialism died when Bernie lost the Democratic primary to Hillary Clinton. But then it was reborn with the stunning upset victory of Alexandria Ocasio-Cortez! But it died again when she failed to overthrow capitalism . . . until it came back when the Democratic Socialists of America reached 100,000 members. And then something else happened and, apparently, it's totally dead again.

You see, now that socialism is a relevant force in US society for the first time in a hundred years, it gets to experience the celebrity cycle of twenty-first-century news coverage. In the blink of an eye, socialist candidates, organizations, and policies like Medicare for All and the Green New Deal have gone from being exciting newcomers to tired has-beens. The backlash has predictably been even quicker for Black socialists and other radicals who have pushed to abolish and defund the police—which started being dismissed for lacking majority support about five seconds after most people were first introduced to this radical idea during the 2020 Black Lives Matter rebellion. This book is for people who want to get beneath shallow trends and take a deeper look at what socialism is—but not so deep that you need to be an expert on politics, history, and economics to follow along.

So let's start with a simple statement: Capitalism is a terrible idea. Imagine if we start a society on an uninhabited tropical island, and I propose that the people who do all the work will be paid as little as possible while the people who don't do anything but own stocks in coconut trees will have more money than they could possibly spend in their lifetimes. You would all start looking at one another and shaking your heads. "Wait, wait, hear me out," I might say. "We'll also treat air, water, plants, and animals as objects to be exploited even more ruthlessly than workers!" Now you'd slowly back away because there's obviously something not right with me, even as I continue on: "Wait, don't go! We'll hoard vaccines and wealth and build border walls to keep out the poor. We'll maintain peace with massively destructive weapons and safety with trigger-happy cops and brutal prisons. Why is everybody leaving?"

Here in the USA, home of the world's most billionaires and bankruptcies from medical bills, growing numbers are concluding that there has to be something better than this. Thousands are joining socialist organizations. Millions vote for candidates who proudly call themselves socialists. But what exactly does that mean? It's a lot easier to know what we're against than what we're for, especially when what we're against is the only thing we've ever known. What if opposing capitalism is as pointless as opposing gravity, mortality, or Maroon 5? If we can't describe the alternative we're fighting for, we're just daydreaming—or, if you've got my personality, whining. Capitalism isn't going to collapse just from people complaining about it—even if it can sometimes feel like it on a really good Twitter day.

The last economic order to be permanently overthrown was the system of plantation slavery that powered the world economy for nearly four hundred years. A key turning point took place when hundreds of thousands of enslaved people on the island of Saint-Domingue escaped their plantations, formed an army, defeated repeated invasions from France and Spain, and created the nation of Haiti in 1810. For hundreds of years before the Haitian Revolution, enslaved people had escaped from and risen up against their unjust condition. But without a clear vision of an alternative to the existing order, most of these uprisings aimed to find a way to live outside of plantation slavery, not to overthrow the entire system. The Haitian example changed everything. Across the Americas, what had once been scattered acts of rebellion became after 1810 successive steps toward abolition.

There has not yet been a socialist Haiti to shine a light toward the path out of capitalism. Instead, there have been bright but brief revolutionary flickers, leaving us with inspiration and also arguments about why they were extinguished. No book can match the lived experience of successful revolution in proving that there is something better than capitalism. My more modest aim is to help some of the dreamers and whiners out there start learning what that something better might be.

What is socialism? A short answer is a society whose top priority is meeting all of its people's needs—ranging from food, shelter, and health care to art, culture, and companionship. In contrast, capitalism only cares about any of that stuff to the extent that money can be made off it. But the short answer isn't enough, and I'm only *partly* saying that because I see you skimming these first few pages hoping you don't have to read the whole thing.

Sure, socialism is both more rational and moral than capitalism, but the question has always been if it is practical and attainable. That requires a longer answer. My pitch for you to read the rest of this book is that it will introduce you to the different aspects of socialism—its analysis of capitalism, the main forces that can lead us to a different world, strategies for how to get there, a history of socialist movements and revolutions, and the important questions and debates that we could use your help in trying to figure out.

All that in a little over two hundred pages, which is barely longer than any of the "Terms and Conditions" you probably "approved" sometime in the last week. Unlike Google, I want you to actually read the following pages because I'm not trying to trick you into signing away whatever rights to privacy you have left. That's just one of the many supposed crimes of socialism that capitalism perfected long ago.

This is a good time to explain who exactly I mean by *we* and *you*. You, of course, are my brilliant and attractive reader. (Seriously, have you been working out? You look great.) To sharpen my focus, I am imagining that you care deeply about the world, are fairly new to politics, and that, at least until recently, didn't consider yourself a socialist. Others probably called you a liberal, which is a word that today is often used to simply mean anybody who isn't a conservative. As a result, millions of very different people find themselves classified as liberals by default: people without homes and billionaires with nine of them; protesters against bombs and generals who drop them. It's a confusing word that often creates confused politics.

One of the things I want to convince you of is that if you agree with the critique, the theory, and the vision put forward in this book, you're not a liberal but a socialist, and those two terms encompass very different politics. Liberalism can agree with socialism that some things in this society should be reformed, and socialists can and should work alongside liberals to win those changes and block the rising danger of the far right. Where we differ is that liberalism views reforms as ways to preserve capitalism while socialism sees them as steps toward replacing it.

(That reminds me, by *we*, I mean the socialist movement in general, which for the sake of my mental wellness I will imagine as a supportive talk show audience laughing at my jokes, applauding my analysis, and being extremely forgiving when I fall short in explaining our internal disagreements.)

If you do keep reading, you'll have many questions and probably some disagreements too. I'll make suggestions—sometimes in the main text, other times in a footnote—about other sources that go deeper into various topics. For example, maybe you now want to learn more about the Haitian Revolution, which for some strange reason is not part of school curriculums in a country founded by slave owners. I recommend *The Black Jacobins*, an inspiring and beautifully written history by the West Indian socialist, historian, cricket player, sportswriter, and most-interesting-man-in-the-world candidate C. L. R. James. Please read those footnotes, by the way, as they contain not just book recommendations but also silly tangents, hilarious jokes, and—in our very first footnote—a helpful tip on where to find the tastiest $15 artisanal donuts.*

Finally, a word about my tone, which can seem oddly lighthearted for a book about overthrowing capitalism. It's possible that there hasn't been a socialist book with this many jokes since V. I. Lenin's *Big Bathroom Book of Bolshevik Humor*.† The wisecracks aren't just sugar to help the political medicine go down—they're part of the politics. Capitalism is destructive and inhuman, but it's also ridiculous and mocking its absurdities reminds us that a system this dumb can't possibly be indestructible.

We should be able to make fun of ourselves as well. Politicians can dress up every two-bit proposal about corporate tax breaks with big ideas about freedom and liberty—let the radicals who actually have big ideas put them out with a humility and humor befitting those whose dreams still far outpace our accomplishments. Jokes are a precaution against the negativity that is an occupational hazard for activists who spend their lives organizing against war, climate change, and all the other horrors most people try to avoid contemplating for too long. We're looking for a positive path for humanity, not trying to add to the relentless chorus of cranks and trolls.

In other words, later to the haters. Socialism is for lovers.

---

* In hell. *Rim shot!* I'll be down here all book. Try the veal.

† "How many Cossacks does it take to screw in a light bulb?"
Pause for peasants to debate the matter, elect a village committee, and respond, "We don't know. How many?"
"None, because Tsar Nicholas II is a vicious tyrant and most rural villages lack electricity!" I guess you had to be there.

2040: A COLD DAY IN PHILADELPHIA

"Okay, shut up," you hoarsely whisper. "I'm awake." The voice recognition system in your bed recognizes your grouchy Early Day tone and shuts off the alarm. It's one of those old "smart" beds that records details about your sleeping habits, but of course, it's been through the "Stop Snitchin'!" recall so it's no longer connected to the creepy servers that were used to collect people's personal data in the final days of money-power.

But who cares about any of that? It's 4:30 in the freaking morning on the first Tuesday of the month: your day to help open the restaurant. The only thing worse than working Early Day is working Early Day on a Tuesday, the beginning of the workweek. It's nice that we've gotten rid of so many of the old pointless jobs of capitalism (public relations, investment banking, border patrollers, and so on) and distributed the work that actually needs to get done so that most people just work Tuesdays through Thursdays. (Honestly, you don't know how people got anything done when they only had two days off from work. Where did they find the time to learn new languages and take psychedelic drugs?) But you're not exactly in a grateful mood this early on a cold-ass February morning.

Out of the warm bed you go, stretching quietly to not wake up the person still sleeping. (In the interests of making this fantasy as appealing as possible, I'll let you fill in the details about who's in your bed.) You stumble down the hall to the bathroom, still feeling your way around this funky old Victorian house. It's a three-monther that you signed up for with some new friends from the restaurant. You barely knew them before moving in, but it's going pretty well.

Many people choose to live in one permanent place the old-fashioned way—especially older folks and those who experienced the trauma of homelessness, which is now considered a bygone horror, like smallpox or bubonic plague. One of the first post-revolution priorities for city and neighborhood assemblies was to create well-built and pleasant housing for all who needed it out of the millions of houses, mansions, and offices that had previously been abandoned, underused, or stupidly used (public relations, investment banking) . . .

But in recent years there has been a growing desire to break out of the "suffocating prison of sameness," as one viral video put it. The movement for varied housing was born out of fevered debates in assemblies in Seoul and then Tenochtitlán (or "Mexico City," as your mom insists on calling it). When these initial proposals failed to win majorities, organizers created the #MixItUp! campaign, which involved everything from unauthorized apartment swaps to protests outside neighborhood housing offices to creating that ridiculous "Everybody Moooove" song that still sometimes pops in your head.

Within a few months, teenager committees were voting overwhelmingly (and, truth be told, a little bit sneeringly) to demand that varied housing be made available. As has often been the case under socialism, the teens got what they wanted and they turned out to be mostly right, and lately people of all ages have been signing up for residence slots ranging from two months to two years. The resulting shift of housing stock from perm to temp has of course created a lot more administrative, design, and hygiene work for the housing sector. But many #MixItUp! participants understood this would be the case and signed up for jobs in housing to meet the need that they had created.

You've never worked in housing, which is surprising because sometimes it seems like you've worked every possible job. You aren't even thirty and already you've been a kindergarten teacher, an urban wildfire fighter, an elder story recorder, and, most recently, a worker at the plant that retrofits old appliances and smartphones that were designed to consume as much energy as possible and then break down within five years. You loved the mental challenge of that job, figuring out how to salvage something socially useful from those old pieces of profit-maximizing crap. You know that before freedom, working in a factory meant being largely a machine yourself, and that you wouldn't have been able to take extra time on the especially tricky ones—and you definitely wouldn't have been allowed to use some of the extra junk to create goofy monsters made of Segway scooters and espresso pods, a few of which still stand outside the bathrooms. Still, after two years among the toxic chemicals and planet-hating plastic of capitalist consumer goods, you were ready for a change.

A few of your friends are "lifers," but you don't understand why anyone would tie themselves to one job for ten or twenty years. Many young people feel the same way, which isn't great for sectors, like shoreline engineering and trauma research, that require long-term expertise and time commitments. The issue is constantly being argued about online, as well as in elected assemblies, street gatherings, and everywhere else.

Like most people, you've gone to school during and between most of these jobs, taking and teaching classes in biology, basketball, and kink. You even found yourself, much to your surprise, elected a neighborhood spokesperson during the statewide referendum on whether everyone really needs to know algebra. It's ironic how much your life superficially resembles that of many young people in the last decades of capitalism: bouncing around between temporary jobs while also squeezing in time to take classes.

But from what the old-timers have told you, people back then did all that not out of interest, but from desperation to try to find a way out of dead-end jobs that didn't pay rent. That's a strange idea to you—the threat of not having a place to stay or enough to eat. If you woke up late today there would be a lot of people mad at you and you'd feel bad, but you wouldn't worry about not having food or a place to stay. That would be like being afraid of someone flicking a switch that could cut off the supply of air to your lungs. In any case, that's enough daydreaming in the shower. Time to go to work.

It's a typical February morning in Philadelphia, which means very little. Ever since the average temperature increase passed the 2.5-degree Fahrenheit red line, there's been no such thing as typical weather. Yesterday it was 65 degrees. Today it's 40 degrees colder. The pace of planetary burning has slowed down since oil, coal, and gas were phased out in the late twenties, but in 2039 the damage is done. It's a good thing people work three days a week instead of five because there are always neighbors who need help recovering from the latest storm or flood, and . . . wait, did you say 2039 again? It's crazy that it's already 2040!

A couple blocks from home you hop on an express tram zipping toward Center City. The atmosphere is perversely fun as the riders and driver loudly grumble about how much they hate Early Day and argue whether it's worse than Late Day. As you approach downtown on Patti LaBelle Drive, the mood lifts as you all watch the sun rising over the Schuylkill River.

It takes about the same time to reach downtown as it would have in a personal car twenty years ago. The extra minutes spent picking up passengers along the way are offset by having barely any traffic or stoplights. Most city roads became private car–free ten years ago, so the only vehicles on the Patti this morning are trams, delivery and utility trucks, and the occasional ambulance. One of the unanticipated benefits was the windfall of space where all the parked cars used to be. Block committees gleefully tore up the asphalt to plant grass and put out lawn chairs, sculpture gardens, and—in one notorious hipster neighborhood—rows of ironic beer pong tables. Your old block committee planted an herb garden, and you often return there to pick rosemary and cilantro.

(The debate over banning cars, by the way, lasted for years after tram lines were laid across the city—at times it was quite bitter. Car lovers were a minority, but a passionate one. They were not persuaded by the argument that they could still go out for drives on highways and were only appeased—mostly—when the city assembly agreed to convert some of the old roads in Fairmount Park into a driving course. Some of them still rant about having to bike or tram a few miles to get to the lots that hold private cars, but the social media refs have done great work giving them the space to vent while keeping things from getting too nasty.)

You get to work just in time to help open up. After setting up the kitchen you grab some coffee and a muffin and sit down at a small table against the wall. Some mornings you like to join the social diners at one of the long tables, but you're a little preoccupied today so you finish breakfast quickly and get back to the kitchen. Work is busy, not because there are more diners than usual but because a bunch of them have been wheeled over from an elder center and need to be served in the old-fashioned style at their tables rather than just getting food from the kitchen themselves. You don't mind—it's fun actually—but it means you've got to hustle, especially when the three classes of eight-year-olds come in at eleven to learn how to make oatmeal cookies.

That was your favorite part of grade school—the weekly trips to different workplaces. You were the first third grader to figure out how to splice a fiber-optic cable, and the slowest at climbing up and down the manhole ladders. It still blows your mind that before socialism people under a certain age had to sit in school all day without ever seeing work, and people above that age had to do the opposite. When the kids came in, they were surprisingly subdued—in the morning they had heard a presentation from two Afghan parents about the American War—but once they got their hands in the batter they were shrieking and laughing as usual.

The day goes by quickly and happily, until you screw up just as you're getting ready to leave after the lunch rush. Once again, you forgot to charge someone for her meal. Each year the whole money thing feels increasingly pointless in a society in which everyone has more than enough of what they need and plenty of what they want. But it's still the main way for planning committees to allocate energy credits and keep track of how goods and services are being distributed and used. Thanks in part to your forgetfulness, the restaurant had only a vague estimate of how much food it served in January, which pissed off some assemblies and committees because there's a friendly competition going on with New York City to reduce transportation costs and electricity consumption from excess food shipments. Okay, it's not so friendly. Even under socialism, Philly hates New York.

After your sheepish exit from work, you hop on a bike from a nearby lot to go see your uncle. To ease your guilt about the money screwup, you calculate how much electricity you're putting into the city reserves via the bike's kinetic energy charger, but it doesn't help your mood. This visit, which you're doing to get your mom off your back, has been putting you on edge all day. Uncle Mike is a die-hard "profitist." Before the revolutions he was a rising young pharmaceutical executive who found it impossible to reconcile himself to the radical democracy of mass assemblies that replaced the Wall Street/Pentagon regime. He worked alongside other profitists to sabotage the new system, organizing medicine shortages in city hospitals. People died because of Uncle Mike and he was sentenced to ten years in one of Pennsylvania's prisons. (A common joke in those early years was that socialism had gentrified the jails because they had become so much richer and whiter.) He was released a few years early along with the other inmates and now he runs a crank profitist website and gets together with old friends in a coffee shop—which they insist on still calling "Dunkin' Donuts"—to mutter about how much better things used to be.

Your visit is short and unpleasant, with Uncle Mike spending the whole time on one of his rants. Today his anger is focused on the reparations commission. How could they rename the Vine Street Expressway after Mumia Abu-Jamal, the radical Black political prisoner whose books you read in school? And how is it fair that African Americans must make up more than half of all elected bodies in the city? That's a violation of democracy! You know that your uncle has never cared about democracy. What he's upset about is the sight of Black people running a city for real—not like in the old days when there could be Black mayors but real power was with wealthy white people like Uncle Mike.

You try to stay calm and reasonable, pointing out that if it weren't for the Black prison abolitionists, he'd still be in jail. He ignores you and you want to blurt out that you worry they're wrong, that they don't know people like your uncle the way you do. You see every time there's a blackout or fruit shortage, he and his Dunkin' buddies put out lies that it's because socialism isn't working, even though they know full well that supply chains were collapsing under the strain of droughts and epidemics toward the end of money-power.

You don't wish him more suffering than he's already had, but you also don't like him and don't fully understand why you are supposed to see him. This question offends your mother: he is your family; no other explanation is necessary. But she has to know this isn't true, that the definition of family has never been more flexible. Just last month you were part of a kin commemoration with an old firefighter friend where you pledged lifetime support and were added to one another's crisis support lists. You've done the same with a few other friends, your favorite teacher, some of the kids at the 24-hour child-care center where you take shifts, most of your cousins, and your siblings.

You haven't bothered to ask your mom because it's unnecessary and you know she'll feel insulted. In general, the only ones her age who get it are like your Aunt Olivia, who has told you that queer people always had to create what they called "chosen families." Aunt Olivia has cut off Uncle Mike, which your mom can't abide. She may hate the things he's done, but she still believes that when all is said and done, the only people you can count on are your biological relatives. So the three of you argue.

On your way home from your uncle's, you wonder if there are more arguments under socialism. It can be tedious for every major decision to be democratically decided, especially when there are no easy answers. The question about keeping stores open twenty-four hours, for example, which pits a minor convenience for many consumers against a more substantial sacrifice for a small number of workers, has been reversed multiple times over the years.

Everything is being rethought and redesigned at the same time—nobody wants to be told to hold off on their new ideas so that at least we can have some continuity somewhere, and the results are often confusion, sometimes chaos, which Uncle Mike's website calls "dumb-unism." You strongly disagree, but you have to admit that it's sometimes exhausting to constantly question old assumptions and habits, and to not have the false reassurance that everything will be okay because the people in charge are wiser than you. You think that socialism is a bit like what your mom says about parenthood: a new world of responsibilities that are sometimes overwhelming but also impossible to imagine not having. Personally, you find it quite easy to picture life without your own kids, but not one without the joys and burdens of being an active participant in deciding what kind of world you live in.

Older folks can have an especially hard time with the new responsibilities, but even you sometimes tune everything out for a couple of weeks and just go around with your headphones on, like those pictures of people from the last years of capitalism. Of course, you know that back then people got into lots of arguments too, much worse than the ones today because they weren't aimed at solving anything but just blaming each other for the problems they had no power to fix.

Maybe you'll drop by a philosophy discussion tonight—there's a Tuesday one at a bar in your neighborhood—to bounce some of these ideas around. But first, you think as you pull up in front of your beautiful Victorian three-monther, it is time for a well-deserved Early Day nap.

And . . . scene. There you have it: one fairly crappy socialist day. I thought it would be fun to imagine how much better a socialist world could be even on a relatively bad day. When I was a kid, Ice Cube used this method in reverse when he rapped "Nobody I know got killed in South Central LA / today was a good day" and ever since I've wanted to be known as the Cube of communism.

More importantly, I want to establish from the jump that socialism is more than Medicare for All, the Green New Deal, abolishing ICE, and all the other urgently needed policy changes that have inspired millions of people to support socialist candidates and organizations. It's a world without a small minority that owns and controls our wealth and resources—a phase of history that we haven't yet reached—and so it takes some imagination to wrap our heads around.

That doesn't mean it's a utopia with nothing but harmony and good vibes. The first objection that is often raised against socialism is that it will fall apart at the first sign of disagreement. If I want cars to be banned and housing to be varied, but you want to go on driving and owning a permanent home, mayhem will ensue, followed by bedlam, culminating in downright pandemonium.

This argument, which at its heart is a claim that ordinary people aren't capable of democracy in any society, is bunk. It's true that there might be more daily disagreement—perhaps even some dysfunction—in a society in which so many more people have a say in their life conditions. But this is quite minor compared to the turmoil of being overworked and subject to unjust laws that human beings have grown accustomed to in the name of "order" over a relatively recent period of our species' history.

My hypothetical day can't really tell us anything about socialism—other than the fact that I seem to think it will be written in italics. Socialism isn't a planned community that can be created in advance but the society that humanity will figure out for itself once it is freed from the profit-centric rules of capitalism. But when you're trapped inside capitalist structures that keep relentlessly expanding and blocking out views of alternative ways of life it's not a total waste of time to dream a bit about what concrete forms genuine democracy and equality could take.

People have pursued the dream of a world based on cooperation for thousands of years. Some have given up all their money and joined monasteries. Others have spent lots of money and gone to Burning Man. The unique contribution of socialism, starting with its modern founder Karl Marx, is the idea that the working class could be a force that brings this about for everyone, not just for a few people dropping out of society to join a commune.

Workers have this potential because of their numbers and economic power, and more importantly because the only way they can successfully take on their bosses is to organize collectively. I didn't come up with those committees and councils in my make-believe socialist day scenario out of thin air. They have been created in countless workers' revolutions and uprisings over the past century and a half. The future steps we take toward socialism won't be formed out of the minds of today's socialists but out of the decisions made by tomorrow's workers in the course of their fight for freedom.

But some inspiration is necessary to see how we might get to a hopeful future from a dismal present. "Look at the movies that we see all the time," radical philosopher Slavoj Žižek told the crowd at the Occupy Wall Street protest encampment in 2011. "It's easy to imagine the end of the world—an asteroid destroying all of life, and so on—but we cannot imagine the end of capitalism." Ten years, a global pandemic, and many hurricanes and wildfires later, it's common to not only imagine the end of the world but to believe that we are living it.*

And still we struggle to envision an alternative. Climate scientists prove time and again that our economic structures are driving most species to extinction but can't model how these structures can be overturned. Facts and research aren't enough to successfully challenge the only way of life we've ever known. We need imagination to show how different the world can be, and we need power to make that world a reality. Socialists are ultimately judged by how well they can get those two wild horses, power and imagination, to run in the same direction.

Revolutionaries have long warned about capitalism's civilization-

* Are we? More on that in the next chapter.

threatening tendencies—most famously when the great Polish socialist Rosa Luxemburg warned that society faced a choice of "either transition to socialism or regression into barbarism." But socialism is about more than avoiding Armageddon. It's also about finally freeing humanity's potential from a system that keeps our immense resources in only a few hands. It was in that spirit that Marx wrote that the end of capitalism would mark the closing of the "prehistory of human society."

Yes, socialism is urgently needed to prevent the demise of human civilization. But it's also needed to begin a new one more worthy of the name.

PART I

THE END?

CROATOAN

1.

ALL IS NOT LOST

Books like this often begin by describing just how awful everything has gotten under capitalism. But is that really what you want? Aren't you already feeling stressed out enough?

Anxiety levels have been steadily rising during this era of unapologetic racism, unrestrained police violence, and unbridled corporate greed—and that was before the COVID pandemic and accelerated pace of fires and floods pushed the public sense of panic to a seeming all-time high. At this point, hearing bad news can be paralyzing. If I start in on you right away with depressing tales of extreme poverty and mass extinctions, I'm afraid you'll be less likely to take to the streets than crawl under your sheets.

A 2021 survey from the online activist organization Avaaz found that 84 percent of young people around the world were at least somewhat worried about climate change. Almost half were so anxious that it "affected their daily life and functioning," with even higher numbers in the poorer countries facing the heaviest impact of rising storms and ocean levels. It used to be that the only people talking about the end of the world were cult leaders, goth kids, and street corner prophets holding signs that read "The End Is Nigh." Now we all can get lost for hours staring silently at our phones while doomscrolling—a word that in my childhood would only have existed as the name of that one weird dystopian song on every album in the 1980s, the one written by the drummer after he got high and watched *Blade Runner.** In the 2020s, if you want to freak people out, stand on the corner with a sign declaring "Everything's Going to Be Great!" Within minutes you'll be surrounded by news vans, social workers, and a SWAT team.

Brooding over the apocalypse has become the opposite of edgy: it's Disney. The corporation that once sold us fairy tales about one day marrying Prince Charming now creates precise CGI renderings of interplanetary Armageddon. There is no "Circle of Life" when every character in *Star Wars: Rogue One* is vaporized by the world-destroying Death Star, and Thanos destroying half of all life in the universe in *Avengers: Infinity War* is the grimmest possible realization of the old song "It's a Small World (After All)."

When even Disney has gone dark, it's clear that doom is becoming its own kind of dominant narrative. These movies (some of which are great) connect to our feelings about living in a world under constant threat, but they'll never seriously explore solutions that might threaten their own revenue streams, which is why we don't see superheroes vaporizing oil pipelines or SHIELD agents forming a union.

Most of us spend our days marinating in this sense of dread. Whether your preferred strategy for dread is to ignore, obsess, or aggressively deny, chances are you find it hard to think coherently about the underlying issues for much more than thirty seconds. In fact, I don't think we're quite ready for it now. So let's take a quick historical detour, all the way back to 1587 and the so-called "Lost Colony of Roanoke." It's a story you may have heard about another society that was doomed—only it's a lie. Roanoke was never lost at all. It was found, saved, and adopted by Indigenous neighbors. This is a history with a happy ending, but it's one that doesn't promote capitalism and colonialism, and so the guardians of American culture simply erased it, replacing it with a version that ends in disaster and apocalypse. Sound familiar?

---

* Other everyday phrases that would have terrified young Danny include "ICE agent," "content provider," and "smart toaster."

* * *

Roanoke was the first English settlement in North America, on the Outer Banks of what is today known as North Carolina. English settlers arrived in 1587 with a belief in their right to claim any land they "discovered" in the Americas. A hundred years earlier, the pope had granted Spain and Portugal this right—which became known as the Doctrine of Discovery—so they could spread the Christian faith and demonstrate to the clueless Natives who stewarded and honored the land that in fact the Lord meant for His Earth to be conquered, fenced off, and sucked dry of its nutrients and metals.*

The 115 colonists were excited to demonstrate this superior European knowledge of land use but were held back by their stunning lack of actual knowledge of the land. The funder of the Roanoke expedition, Sir Walter Raleigh, thought that on the other side of the Outer Banks was not a giant continent but the Pacific Ocean, which would make Roanoke an excellent pit stop for ships making their way to China. Raleigh also seemed to think the area was home to mythical creatures and fabulous riches, because that's what the Spanish had once been told by a local Native they kidnapped—not realizing that the poor guy was telling them whatever they wanted to hear so they would eagerly sail back to his home and he could escape, which is exactly what he did.†

The colonists must have been disappointed to find a narrow and scrubby beach that was extremely far from China and lacked a single silver-pooping llama, or whatever weird stuff they were promised

---

* I generally use *Indigenous* to describe the original and rightful inhabitants of the Americas, but I occasionally use *Native Americans* or *Indians*, all of which are used by Indigenous activists and authors. None of these terms are ideal, which is unsurprising given that it's the language of genocidal colonizers.

† History didn't get this guy's name, but what a baller, right? I hope he made it all the way back to his people, but if he did, I'm worried they treated him like someone claiming to be abducted by aliens: "Listen, we all want to believe you, but you're telling us that these people across the sea ride giant deer, have skin the color of bird shit, and never, ever bathe?"

by Sir Walter. Like settlers everywhere, they depended on the expertise and goodwill of Indigenous neighbors, so when they mistakenly attacked their Native allies from the nearby island of Croatoan because they thought they were a different group of Indians (facepalm) they considered hostile, they knew they were screwed.

The colonists sent their governor John White back to England to get more supplies and reinforcements. Bad weather and a naval war with Spain delayed White's return by three years. When he finally arrived, he found Roanoke completely abandoned, with only one silent indication of the colonists' fate. At the center of the abandoned site was a word, carved into a wooden post: CROATOAN.

We know from Governor White's journal that the colonists said that if they decided to leave their failing settlement, they would carve into a post the location of where they went. Thus, when White returned and saw the sign, he was pretty sure they had gone to Croatoan, where apparently they still had some relationships even after the unprovoked attack. Over the following centuries many Native people in the region would tell histories of the Roanoke colonists being taken in and assimilated by their Indigenous neighbors, claims that are being confirmed by archeologists.* While there is some debate about where exactly the colonists went, the basic story is clear. They gave up waiting for an English supply ship, put their fate in the hands of people who could survive even when the stuff they ordered didn't get delivered, and they lived. Hooray!

But school textbooks and TV shows continue to tell tales of a "lost colony" that was either murdered by Indians or simply vanished in the wild dark forests of the mysterious new world. It's a legend that was created in the early 1800s for a new United States that wanted national folklore, and it later grew in popularity in a post–Civil War South that needed stories of white victimhood and dark-skinned sav-

---

* I got much of the Roanoke story from Andrew Lawler's *The Secret Token: Myth, Obsession, and the Search for the Lost Colony of Roanoke*. But for a better understanding of how many Indigenous people understand the history, I recommend Malinda Maynor Lowery's *The Lumbee Indians: An American Struggle*.

agery. "Lost Colony" legends have made Roanoke Island a tourist destination and the subject of schlocky History Channel episodes about supernatural forces and alien abductions.

Minus the goofy *X Files* stuff, this narrative is actually mainstream history. In his classic colonial history *American Slavery, American Freedom*, for example, Edmund Morgan writes that the Roanoke colonists "simply disappeared, presumably killed by the Indians. What was lost in this famous lost colony . . . and never quite recovered in subsequent ventures was the dream of the Englishman and Indian living side by side in peace and liberty."

Why was an eminent historian like Morgan unable to see the clear evidence that the English and Indians did end up living together in peace and liberty? Perhaps because it happened under the Indian leadership and therefore "simply disappeared" into a world outside of American history. Instead, this distinguished Yale professor opts for the John Wick version of history, where a colonist in the middle of a massacre crawls over to a post so that he can painstakingly carve the word CROATOAN—presumably while he's moaning from the pain of arrows in his back.

The "Lost Colony" is a good campfire story. It's creepy to imagine walking into an abandoned village with a mysterious word carved into a tree, even if the carving was actually just a sixteenth-century version of a Post-It note left on the fridge. But the real history of Roanoke is much more interesting. Facing their own version of the end of the world, the colonists were forced to discard the Doctrine of Discovery, European supremacy, and surely many other assumptions they had long considered plain common sense.

Was there a debate? Did some of them choose to die rather than submit to Native rule? Why did the Croatoan take in people who had attacked them? Did they demand some measure of reparations? Then there are the larger counterfactual questions about what might have happened if other settlements had followed Roanoke's path. What kind of societies could have emerged in North America borne out of collaboration rather than genocide? And what kind of a different world could we be living in four hundred years later? We'll never know those answers, but what we can and must know is that other histories were possible, then and now. That's an important lesson at a time when our inability to adapt is threatening to make all of humanity a lost colony.

* * *

Okay, now it's time for the scary stuff. I started writing this chapter on the eve of the Climate Change Summit in Glasgow, Scotland, when the United Nations reported that even if governments fulfill their current pledges to reduce carbon dioxide emissions, global temperatures are set to rise by 2.7 degrees Celsius (almost 5 degrees Fahrenheit). That's almost double the 1.5-degree threshold that scientists agree is the absolute limit before rising ocean levels, deadly heatwaves, and dwindling food supplies pose serious challenges to largescale human civilization.

The only thing more frightening than rising temperatures is our immobility in the face of it, like the nightmare of being frozen in place with an oncoming truck bearing down on you. The crisis is often discussed as something recently discovered, but a US government advisory committee way back in 1965 warned about "marked changes in climate" from rising levels of carbon dioxide in the atmosphere. The first UN climate summit happened in 1992, before many of you were born. Glasgow was the twenty-sixth summit, which means it was also the twenty-sixth consecutive time scientists gathered from around the world and were ignored. There's a reason why the phrase "twenty-seventh time's the charm!" doesn't exist.

It's so bad we can't even accurately name the problem. How the hell can we organize a historic fight against ecological collapse using pleasantries like *climate change* and *global warming*? The same politicians who casually scapegoat vast numbers of people as *terrorists* or *criminals* feel the need to be remarkably polite to the atmospheric elements choking our planet to death. I suggest we follow the lead of Muscogee scholar Daniel Wildcat and call it "global burning." After all, Wildcat asks, what else makes sense for a process that starts with the burning of fossil fuels and ends with flames engulfing entire ecosystems?*

* Wildcat's *Red Alert: Saving the Planet with Indigenous Knowledge* is a

In the Avaaz survey about climate anxiety, 60 percent of young people reported feeling betrayed and abandoned by adults and governments. Believe me, kids, we're disgusted with ourselves too. Our obvious failure to protect future generations produces vast amounts of contempt for ourselves, our societies, and our democracies. Self-loathing is almost as big a part of our culture today as fear. It produces nasty politicians who are skilled at manipulating this self-hate into scapegoating others.

Why is it such a struggle for us to steer ourselves out of the way of this oncoming civilizational car crash? One popular explanation is that human beings are a planet-destroying species by nature. This is the Agent Smith Theory. Smith is the AI program deployed in *The Matrix* to hunt down the people trying to resist being colonized and destroyed. Here's the speech he gives while torturing the leader of the resistance:

> I tried to classify your species and I realized that you're not actually mammals. Every mammal on this planet instinctively develops a natural equilibrium with the surrounding environment, but you humans do not. You move to an area and you multiply and multiply until every natural resource is consumed and the only way you can survive is to spread to another area. There is another organism on this planet that follows the same pattern. Do you know what it is? A virus. Human beings are a disease, a cancer of this planet.

As with all great villain monologues, most of the audience find ourselves being at least half convinced. And in fact, there are many environmental scientists who argue that we should name our current geological era the Anthropocene—"anthro" being a prefix for human to indicate that this is an era defined by the fact that human activity is destabilizing the planet. But the problem with this theory is that our species has been around for hundreds of thousands of years, while the era of destabilization referred to as the Anthropocene is at most two hundred years old—coincidentally just about as old as the spread of industrial capitalism.*

---

short, often funny book that has had an outsized impact on my thinking.

* There are a number of socialist scientists who for that reason argue we should actually call this era the Capitalocene.

We have been unable to stop global burning because of capitalism—not its technology but its upside-down rules and priorities. It's a global order where those with enough wealth and power to privately own something—such as enough underground fossil fuels to wipe out humanity if they are burned into the atmosphere—can do whatever they want with it. All the rest of us—99.99 percent of humanity and 100 percent of other lifeforms—can do is to beg them not to.

Unlike the Roanoke colonists, we have never let go of the disastrous Doctrine of Discovery, which the Supreme Court has repeatedly cited as a legal basis for US theft of Indigenous land.* But the order of argument has been reversed. Back then, rich people claimed the right to own other people's land because they knew best how it should be "improved" through relentless exploitation of the soil and those who work it. Today, it's obvious that this supposed "knowledge" has been a monumental disaster, but rich people continue to claim the right to destroy the land because they own it. As long as we play by those rules, we're stuck in a comic book movie where a supervillain threatens to blow up the world—and the superheroes respond with conferences and strongly worded condemnations. Is there not something more we can do?

Of course there is! After all these decades of research and summits and declarations, it may seem that we've exhausted all possible remedies, meetings, and reports and research, but there's one thing we haven't yet tried that I'm pretty sure could work. I don't want to bore you with scientific jargon, but my idea for quickly reducing global burning is to STOP DOING IT. We can STOP BURNING OIL, GAS, and COAL that produce gasses that trap excess heat in the atmosphere, and use the money we save by not digging up the planet and lighting it on fire to build safer energy production using safer energy sources like wind and solar that DON'T.

---

* Starting with the 1823 *Johnson v. M'Intosh* decision and most recently in 2005's *City of Sherrill v. Oneida Indian Nation of N.Y.* It's a common misunderstanding that the Supreme Court's job is to uphold the US Constitution rather than ignorant decrees by medieval popes, but its actual purpose is to grab whatever collection of words it can find as long as they serve to protect the interests of the rich and powerful. If you don't believe me, wait until I tell you about Roscoe Conkling.

The executives and investors who own most of the oil, gas, and coal in the ground are an extremely tiny fraction of the world's population. Some of them might be kind fathers and good friends, but they are also genocidal sociopaths who think it's more important to get the best return on their investment than to worry about poisoning us all. It wouldn't be hard to take away their control of fossil fuels and put them somewhere where they can't continue to cause harm. Such people have obviously been profoundly damaged by capitalism, and might require many years of reflection to recover their humanity.

But to do that requires breaking capitalism's most foundational (and fanatical) rules about the sacredness of rich people's property rights. Recent years have seen historically large protests demanding something be done to stop global burning. Most of humanity doesn't think a few people should be allowed to broil us all just because they own the means of destruction, but we are also hampered by not knowing another way to live. And how could we, when for the last five hundred years all alternative models—from Indigenous societies to socialist revolutions—have been crushed and erased?

Of course, we're up against not just bad ideas and bad vibes but a vast military-financial-industrial complex that simply can't help itself. A 2021 report called *Banking on Climate Chaos* estimated that the world's largest sixty banks invested almost four trillion dollars in fossil fuels . . . in the five years after the 2016 Paris climate agreement that was hailed as a much greater success than Glasgow. That's a terrifyingly massive investment that the world's most powerful people and institutions fully intend to see through and make a profit. If they win their bet, we all lose. The argument of this book is that socialism is our best shot at preventing that from happening.

The apocalypse can happen. It already has, for many people through history. The world ended for most Indigenous people across North America in the centuries after Roanoke, as it did for many Africans in the centuries of the slave trade, as it did for my mother's family and many other Jewish and Roma communities during the Nazi Holocaust. We know from those horrors that the end of the world doesn't mean everyone is vaporized at the snap of a finger. Some people survive, against long odds and carrying tremendous trauma, because our capacity to adapt, rebuild, and love is as incredible as our capacity to hate and destroy. But every time humanity loses so much, not only millions of lives but countless ideas, cultures, and best practices for how to make a better world.

It doesn't have to come to that again. There are two sides to the story of Roanoke. The disturbing side is the "Lost Colony" legend, which shows that our culture would prefer that we all die rather than live in a society without rich and poor and where white people aren't in charge. More inspirational is what actually seems to have happened, a story of adaptation and survival where white people aren't in charge. The real lesson of the history of the Croatoan and the colonists is that there have been and continue to be alternative endings that have been lost to us but can still be found.

We have a real chance to save our world, and to be part of a cast of superheroes more numerous than even Disney can afford. That starts with finding ways to lift one another out of despair. I'm not telling you to be optimistic, to look on the bright side, or God forbid, to smile. What I am saying is that fixating on the end of the world, understandable as that can be, has become as clichéd as a played-out movie franchise.

The truly original idea isn't that humanity is doomed. It's that we can change. So let's go out there are raise some hell, and maybe we can live happily ever after.

2.

GHOST STORIES

A ghost is haunting the United States—the ghost of socialism. All kinds of elites and defenders of the status quo stand united against this demon: presidents and megachurch preachers, Fox News hosts and Facebook censors, Wall Street CEOs and local sheriffs.

Can you name a single Republican who doesn't accuse their Democratic opponent of being part of an evil socialist conspiracy? How many Democrats don't respond by throwing socialists under the bus and claiming to be the only reasonable alternative to left and right extremism? This means two things:

1. *The rich and powerful can see that socialism is a real threat to their way of life.*
2. *Now is the time for socialists to let the people know our real beliefs, goals, and strategies, and replace these childish ghost stories with a clear explanation of the better world we're fighting for.*

How did you like that bold introduction? I kind of stole it from Karl Marx and Friedrich Engels, but it's okay—we're all comrades. Here are the opening lines of their *Communist Manifesto*:

> A spectre is haunting Europe—the spectre of communism. All the powers of old Europe have entered into a holy alliance to exorcise this spectre: Pope and Tsar, Metternich and Guizot, French Radicals and German police-spies.
>
> Where is the party in opposition that has not been decried as communistic by its opponents in power? Where is the opposition

> that has not hurled back the branding reproach of communism, against the more advanced opposition parties, as well as against its reactionary adversaries?
>
> Two things result from this fact:
>
> I. Communism is already acknowledged by all European powers to be itself a power.
>
> II. It is high time that Communists should openly, in the face of the whole world, publish their views, their aims, their tendencies, and meet this nursery tale of the Spectre of Communism with a manifesto of the party itself.

The Communist Manifesto might be the most influential book in the history of the world, if you don't count the ones about God or teenage wizards. Within months of its publication in 1848, revolutions broke out across Europe. Terrified elites thought that the two young authors must have immense powers, either to prophesy uprisings or to create them. In fact, Marx and Engels had no idea that 1848 would become a historic year, but they did know change was in the air because they had been spending a lot of time with pissed-off workers. Which was and still is an unusual habit for intellectuals.

People in Paris, Berlin, and elsewhere didn't rise up that year because Karl Marx told them to. But after they had taken to the streets, the *Manifesto* provided many of them with a vision of what their revolt—and future ones—could achieve. This has been the aim of socialism ever since: to demonstrate how the courage and creativity that people already possess can point the way toward a different society that will be built on those qualities rather than be threatened by them.

For capitalists and their servants, socialism has long been a zombie that just won't die. For almost two hundred years they've had socialists scapegoated, fired, deported, and worse. And then . . . just when they thought it was safe to get back in their yachts . . . there we are again, ghoulishly trying to dismember their mansions and mutilate their inherited wealth.

The *Manifesto*'s introduction feels especially relevant today. The United States in 2023 isn't 1848 Paris, and I don't expect the publication of this book to trigger a revolution (although, wow, how good would that be for getting invited onto podcasts?). But socialism is very much back in the spotlight—and crosshairs. It started with the Occupy Wall Street and Black Lives Matter movements and then burst into full view with the popularity of Bernie Sanders and Alexandria Ocasio-Cortez, the election of dozens of other socialists across the country, and the explosive growth of the Democratic Socialists of America (DSA).

Republicans, whose party symbol is an enormous stomping animal that is terrified at the sight of a mouse, were obsessed with socialism even back when few of us were around, so of course they are freaking out (and fundraising) over the new Red Scare. They demonize Medicare for All as a plot to take away health insurance (huh?) and the Green New Deal as capital punishment for those caught eating a hamburger. I'm surprised some right-wing freedom lover hasn't yet held a press conference to declare traffic lights a communist plot.*

More alarming is the growth of armed militias and delusional mobs that are convinced that everything around them—from vaccine clinics to fourth-grade lesson plans about slavery—is part of a vast communist conspiracy. Social media has accelerated the spread of misinformation, but the sentiment is as old as the first slave patrol. The American Dream has always been to become so rich and powerful that you can spend the rest of your life obsessed that everyone else is out get you. This is a country that produces $20 trillion in wealth each year but freaks out at poor children asking for help at its border, a place where Land Rover shoppers cry tyranny if the dealership receptionist asks them to put on a mask, and police in full body armor fire panicked rounds into unarmed bodies.

Meanwhile, the socialists they are so scared of are often a tame bunch. From Fox News, we learn about our sinister plans for universal uniforms of gray cardigans and gender reassignment surgeries for anyone caught with a copy of the Constitution, and we shrug in confusion at each other in the church basement where we have monthly meetings: "Did you say that? I didn't say that."

---

* For real though, is it just a coincidence that the top light happens to be red? Hey, I'm just asking questions.

The dreaded socialist agenda is actually rather moderate at the moment. Free universal health care is already in place in every other wealthy capitalist country in the world besides the US. Abolishing ICE and Homeland Security just means going back to the way things were before 9/11. The policies that make up the Green New Deal are more unprecedented but still modest first steps compared to radical changes demanded by global burning.

When Bernie ran for president in 2016, one of his most prominent supporters was former labor secretary Robert Reich, who had recently written a book called *Saving Capitalism: For the Many, Not the Few.** It might seem odd that someone who wants to save capitalism would support a candidate who famously calls himself as a socialist. But Reich's vision of a "saved" capitalism was not so far from Sanders's "democratic socialism," which he often described as an expansion of the great capitalist reforms of the twentieth century such as social security and Medicare.

Many conservatives would argue that this proves that Robert Reich is really a socialist, while some leftists might insist that it shows Bernie Sanders really isn't one. To me it just shows that capitalism has corrupted politics to the point that you practically have to be a socialist just to push for the most basic and common-sense reforms. This is a big reason why socialism is gaining support, but it's important to make sure these reforms are seen as our first steps rather than our final goal.

Because few people have had the opportunity to learn what socialism means, much less be involved in a socialist organization, the word can mean almost anything to the left of Joe Rogan. As a result, the word *socialism* is in the air more than it has been in generations, but more as a floating piece of pink crepe paper rather than a bright red flag. That has begun to change as socialist candidates have helped turn programs like Medicare for All and the Green New Deal into what is sometimes called a "minimum program" for socialism. The aim of this book is to build on that minimum, and add some more flesh and blood to socialism's specter.

---

* I don't agree with saving capitalism, but Reich is very good at explaining why the so-called "free market" is actually a set of rules that can and should be changed to benefit the democratic majority.

* * *

Socialism is defined less by specific laws than by who has the power to oversee them. It's about eliminating distinctions between the government and the governed. The reason many people don't support economic and environmental policies that are "in their interest" is that they don't think the politicians and bureaucrats who would implement those policies would ever act in their interest. And it's hard to argue with their experience. That's why a fuller definition of socialism should start with two simple but far-reaching concepts about socialism:

1. Working people control the government.
2. The government controls the economy.

Number 2 has been the main feature of many countries that call themselves socialist or communist, and I just realized how much that sounded like a conservative potty joke.* But it's Number 1—democracy at every level of society—that transforms mere state control of the economy into socialism. Karl Marx, Vladimir Lenin, and Rosa Luxemburg were all freedom fighters living under kings and dictators. They were socialists because they concluded that full democracy was impossible under capitalism. By democracy, they didn't mean having a vote on one day in November, but taking an active part in all of society's important decisions.

Because we are so used to picturing the masters of both government and economy as narrow centralized powers that rule over us from a handful of buildings, it is hard for us to picture changes in society that go beyond replacing the people in those buildings with others who are hopefully more honest and noble. Socialism wouldn't just replace those people but the system that centralizes so much power in a few buildings. It would broaden the bases of decision-making to thousands of buildings and public squares and community centers. It is a system in which the people control the government by changing what government means.

Unlike billionaire dreams of libertarian moon colonies, these ideas have come not from unchecked imaginations and egos but from

---

* By right-wing comedy standards, it's downright brilliant satire. And if you don't agree, I'll whine about being censored.

the concrete experience of popular resistance. Socialists first got a glimpse of revolutionary mass democracy, for example, in 1871, when an uprising in France created the revolutionary citywide assembly known as the Paris Commune. This was a new form of government in which officials were paid no more than the average worker's wage and were immediately recallable if voters were unhappy with them. An excited Karl Marx noted that "instead of deciding once in three years which member of the ruling class was to misrepresent them," the Commune allowed voters to replace those elected as easily as bosses can replace employees in the workplace.*

Just as democracy should exist beyond Election Day, it should also exist outside government buildings. Socialism is about giving people a say in how every aspect of their lives is run, which is not only noble but also more effective. Ten years ago, I got a taste of this potential as a minor participant in Occupy Wall Street. What started as a tiny protest encampment on the doorstep of some of the world's most powerful banks soon sprouted committees that created kitchens, libraries, art, and whatever projects anybody wanted to pursue—from supporting nearby picket lines to challenging deportations and foreclosures. Others have had similar experiences in local mutual aid networks that have sprung up during the COVID pandemic and after natural disasters, as well as in Indigenous-led protest encampments to stop oil pipelines. Many would agree with the Occupy participant who wrote that "the skill and imagination on display mounted ever more as an indictment of the alienated world outside that kept us from sharing what we could do with each other, tricked us into selling our time and talents for money."†

It is this type of radical participatory democracy, functioning as the foundation of a centrally organized political and economic system, that is the heart of the socialist vision. Many older people know that

* Marx unfortunately then added that "it's well known that companies in matters of business generally know how to put the right man in the right place and if they make a mistake to redress it." This might be the most wildly inaccurate thing Marx ever wrote, but for some reason it isn't often used against him by defenders of capitalism.

† This is from Nathan Schneider's "Thank You Anarchy." I share Schneider's gratitude, even if I'm not an anarchist, but I'll get into that in chapter 9.

the name of Russia's "communist" government was the Soviet Union, but few know that *soviet* was Russian for *council*. The Russian Revolution was created and (briefly) led by democratically elected soviets, which sprang up in factories, military barracks, and peasant villages across the country to conduct the revolution in their local areas and elect delegates to the regional and national soviet government.

"No political body more sensitive and responsive to the popular will was ever invented," wrote the great socialist journalist John Reed in 1919 about these unique councils. As with the Paris Commune, delegates to the soviet could be voted out immediately by unhappy voters. Housewives, domestic servants, and other working people who didn't labor in factories could organize themselves into bodies and gain representation in the soviets. Only employers and police were excluded.

Soviets and other democratic working-class bodies have popped up in many other revolutions in the past century, including in Spain in 1936. Here is how George Orwell described Barcelona that year in his thrilling *Homage to Catalonia*:

> Every shop and cafe had an inscription saying that it had been collectivized; even the bootblacks had been collectivized and their boxes painted red and black. Waiters and shop-walkers looked you in the face and treated you as an equal. Servile and even ceremonial forms of speech had temporarily disappeared. Nobody said "Señor" or "Don" or even "Usted"; everyone called everyone else "Comrade" or "Thou," and said "Salud!" instead of "Buenos dias." . . . And it was the aspect of the crowds that was the queerest thing of all. In outward appearance it was a town in which the wealthy classes had practically ceased to exist. Except for a small number of women and foreigners there were no "well-dressed" people at all. Practically everyone wore rough working-class clothes, or blue overalls or some variant of militia uniform. All this was queer and moving. There was much in this that I did not understand, in some ways I did not even like it, but I recognized it immediately as a state of affairs worth fighting for.

You may know George Orwell as the author of *1984* and *Animal Farm,* which are taught in many schools as works of antisocialist propaganda. You probably don't know that Orwell was a socialist who rejected dictatorships that called themselves communist but supported the real thing when he saw it.*

The revolutions in Russia and Spain didn't last. Neither did Occupy Wall Street, for that matter, or Bernie's presidential campaigns. That doesn't prove that the task of socialism is impossible—any more than the history of dozens of failed slave insurrections proved that plantation slavery would never end. But it does mean that we too are haunted, by our fears of the capitalist future but also by the failures of previous generations. These defeats, Marx once wrote, "weigh like a nightmare on the brains of the living," which means that socialists have zombie issues of our own.†

It's often said that socialism has been proven not to work. Some of this is blatant propaganda, like the common right-wing claim that socialism has killed a hundred million people. This strangely round number is arrived at by counting all the victims of horrific famines in the early years of self-proclaimed communist governments in China and the Soviet Union. But anticommunists never do the same math for capitalism. It's estimated that ninety million people die around the world of starvation every single decade—and that's before we include the hundreds of millions who have died from capitalist wars, enslavement, and genocide.

But capitalism's cruel failures don't change the fact that neither "communist" dictatorships nor the limited reforms of "socialist" elected governments have succeeded in creating the liberated democratic societies that Marx and Engels described in the *Manifesto*.‡

---

* Unfortunately, Orwell's rightful mistrust of the authoritarian government that emerged out of the Russian Revolution led him in his final days to send a list of suspected Communists to a secret agency inside the British government—which, if you've read the end of *1984*, you'll know is the most Orwellian ending imaginable.

† The quote is from *The Eighteenth Brumaire of Louis Bonaparte* about the complicated aftermath of the 1848 revolution in Paris. It's a tough read if you don't already know the history, but with some background information it's one of the sharpest and wittiest histories you'll ever find.

‡ "Communism" and "socialism" used to mean the same thing in most contexts for Marx and that's how I treat them in this book. We'll get back to this question in chapter 9.

Socialists don't have all the answers for how to move humanity past capitalism—not if we're being honest. That means that even as our movement is making a historic comeback, we are still relatively weak and timid, especially in the face of a menacing right wing that benefits from an unbalanced political order where a few thousand delusional dingbats seem to carry as much weight as millions of Black Lives Matter protesters. It's exciting to see radical demands enter mainstream discussion, but we're still living in a funhouse mirror world where one side openly plots armed attacks on Capitol buildings and the other wonders if it's allowed to say "defund the police" out loud.

The alarming rise of fascist marches and white supremacist groups has exposed for many some of the deep injustices that have always been at the heart of the American political and economic order. This has both pushed many progressives closer to socialism and made many afraid of radicals taking things too far and creating a backlash. This is a major reason why Bernie Sanders lost the 2020 Democratic nomination to Joe Biden. Bernie was the most popular politician in the country, while Joe was a human version of a fourth-place trophy at a karate tournament (only more bronze and shiny!). But Democratic primary voters chose the guy who stood for doing nothing in the hope that his mediocrity would be less threatening to their neighbors and keep them from voting for Donald Trump. That strategy may have helped win the election for Democrats, but it did nothing to address the deeper issues that got us into the kind of mess that made it even thinkable for Trump to get votes from anyone beyond his fellow superrich creeps on Jeffrey Epstein's frequent flyer plan.

The specific circumstances of the 2020 election may have been unique, but we always face hard choices between hope and fear. Any step toward progressive change—whether through elections, strikes, or protests—inevitably unleashes the vortex of fury, panic, and slander that has always rained down on those who fight for liberty and justice for all, and not just rich white American men.* When our anxiety

* Whenever possible I'm going to try to avoid using "American" to describe anyone from North or South America. If you think I'm being overly "politically correct," imagine how French or Polish people would react if

about triggering this reaction leads us to water down our hopes and lower our demands, it doesn't stop our opponents from growing. It makes their side more confident, our side more timid, and reinforces the tilted logic of a political system where Republicans excitedly welcome delusional conspiracy theorists and Democrats kneecap their most popular members for wanting everyone to have health care.

But it's also true that elites and reactionaries truly do see the specter of socialism everywhere—just as they did when Marx and Engels wrote the *Manifesto*. And there is a reason for that. Among elites there are always some dolts who really think they earned what they have, but there are also smarter ones who are acutely aware that their power and privilege comes from an unjust order. This can often make conservatives more sensitive than liberals to just how vulnerable capitalism really is.*

There is some truth, therefore, in right-wing fears that all social welfare programs carry within them the dangerous germ of socialism. When Republicans preach that we're heading down the fiery road of communist damnation because we're not letting enough people die of hunger and disease (a very un-Christian sermon), they are pointing out that these programs are proof that capitalism cannot meet society's most basic needs.

Here's another example. In 2003, the Supreme Court finally overturned a Texas law that had criminalized gay sex, and the super-conservative justice Antonin Scalia warned that "if moral disapprobation of homosexual conduct is 'no legitimate state interest' . . . what justification could there possibly be for denying the benefits of marriage to homosexual couples?" At the time, no states had legalized same-sex marriage, and many liberal commentators scoffed that Scalia was using scare tactics by raising the farfetched

---

Germany started calling itself "Europe." I blame the founding fathers for having absolutely no imagination—just think, they could have named us the United States of Awesome. Maybe we should just count our blessings they didn't go with Slaveryland.

* Corey Robin's *The Reactionary Mind* analyzes many of the most important right-wing thinkers in modern history to argue that conservative theory is basically "the experience of having power, seeing it threatened, and trying to win it back."

prospect of gay people getting married. But Scalia was right, which for once was a good thing.

Then, as marriage equality laws spread across the country, conservatives shouted that traditional gender roles were being undermined, liberals again dismissed their desperate alarmism, and again the conservatives turned out to have good reason to worry. Same-sex marriage has indeed undermined assumptions not only about sexuality but gender as well. Children and teens especially are far more likely now to dress and think of themselves in the way that feels right to them, and not in accordance with some imagined prehistoric gendered chore wheel where Man = Hunt, Woman = Gather.*

Liberals generally define themselves as the rational middle between extremists on both sides and think that if everyone just listened to reason, there wouldn't be so much conflict. This makes them both annoying at parties and unreliable in struggle—cheering on protests at first, but then, when the backlash inevitably comes, assuming that radicals must have provoked it by pushing for too much too soon. In truth, they are the ones with the wild delusion: that this system merely needs a few repairs here and there, even as it staggers under the weight of ecological collapse and billionaire-funded fascism.

Liberals mock Republicans for being irrationally haunted by the specter of socialist barbarians at the gates. But socialists know that ghosts are real. They are the pale hints of a world beyond the one we can see in our daily lives. Our job is to maintain the courage to keep walking in their direction, even when we're not entirely sure of the way, and to keep reminding one another that we have nothing to lose but our nightmares.

---

* On the other hand, as many exasperated activists would point out, most of the biggest LGBTQ organizations focused on the "respectable" (that is, better for fundraising) issue of marriage equality at the expense of fighting for trans rights. The resulting paradox is that trans and nonbinary people have unprecedented cultural impact but face terrifying legal assaults across the country.

PART II

CAPITALISM

3.

WELCOME TO THE JUNGLE

Capitalism is an economic system that supposedly reflects basic human instincts like competition and selfishness. If I were building a society choosing from aspects of human nature, I'd probably go with love and laughter, but that's not what is meant. Capitalism, we are told, fits the way we used to live when we were wild: dog eat dog, law of the jungle, and all that. But dogs don't eat other dogs, and while jungles have many "laws," such as sustainable ecosystems and individual sacrifice for the good of the colony, I'm pretty sure none of them involve clearcutting acres of trees so that we can build another Cinnabon.

Ever since the theory of species evolution was laid out by Charles Darwin, it has been distorted into a nonsensical justification of capitalism known as "Social Darwinism." Evolutionary theory holds that species are constantly in the process of changing to better adapt to their environment—which itself is also constantly changing. Social Darwinists, on the other hand, proclaim that capitalism can never be changed because "survival of the fittest" is a permanent law of nature.

You can't have it both ways. If capitalism is the result of natural evolution (and it's not), then it's not the perfect system for all time but merely a phase of human history that will be replaced as we adapt to changing circumstances—such as, oh I don't know, our planet being on fire. Social Darwinists want to include certain aspects of evolution and leave out others, just as plantation owners used to want the people they enslaved to hear the Christian parts of the Bible about being meek and turning the other cheek but not the angry older Jewish parts about rising up against Pharaoh and escaping to freedom. Today, we are meant to read the Book of Darwin right up until it gets to the present day and then slam the book shut and shout, "and everybody lived happily ever after—the end!" But there are still more pages in the book—hopefully.

Evolutionary theory offers us a way to understand our connection to other living things on nature's family tree, but it's also a wonderful illustration of a philosophical approach to change and contradiction known as dialectics. Dialectical methods help us see things both as they appear on the surface and as the tumultuous processes taking place underneath that might eventually turn them into something else—sometimes over millennia and sometimes in an instant. A seed is a seed, until one morning it is a plant. A population of apes evolves into a new species of early humans. Societies, as this chapter will try to demonstrate, are also in a process of constant change, usually slow and barely detectable but sometimes explosive as conflicts beneath the surface come bursting out.

Capitalism came into existence through both evolution and revolution in parts of Europe from the 1300s to the 1700s. It emerged out of feudal societies, which featured landowners in castles using peasants to grow food and knights to fight other knights working for other rich guys in castles. The internal conflict inside feudalism that eventually produced capitalism was between these landowners and a growing class of merchants and bankers who generated wealth through trade and investment.* Traders had been around for thousands of years, but these ones happened to live in an era when Europe's conquest of the Americas and enslavement of Africans created unprecedented opportunities to gain wealth and power for those who weren't part of the landowning aristocracy. And that group of merchants and bankers

* There's actually a raging argument among socialist historians about the origins of capitalism. Ellen Meiksins Wood and Robert Brenner argue that it primarily developed not from the merchant class but out of the conflict between lords and peasants, which resulted in a new class of landless laborers who would eventually be forced into factory labor. My take on the debate is that everyone involved is really smart and I can't wait to hear how it turns out.

would start investing that wealth in sugar plantations in the Caribbean and textile factories in England.* This is how Marx put it in *Capital*:

> The discovery of gold and silver in America, the extirpation, enslavement and entombment in mines of the aboriginal population, the beginning of the conquest and looting of the East Indies, the turning of Africa into a warren for the commercial hunting of black-skins, signalised the rosy dawn of the era of capitalist production.

As Marx's bitter (and perhaps demeaning) sarcasm indicates, capitalism exists today not because it is the best of all possible economic systems but because history happened to work out in a certain way—which included some of the greatest crimes in human history.† This fact by itself doesn't prove that capitalism has to go. But it does mean that the notion that capitalism came about "naturally" is either ignorant or a justification of European (and Euro-American) tyranny over the world—as well as the tyranny within Europe of a small capitalist class. This is why efforts to acknowledge the crimes of history, such as by renaming Columbus Day and making Juneteenth a federal holiday to celebrate slavery's end, aren't empty virtue signaling about the distant past, as critics claim, but powerful ways of understanding and beginning to address the injustices of the present.

Capitalism is far from the only system that has produced horrible cruelties. There is little evidence in the historical record of "ethically sourced" pyramids or marble temples. But it's also not the case, as we are often led to believe, that human history before the modern era was just one long violent ignorant mess—minus a few heroic centuries in ancient Greece and Rome. In fact, for most of our existence humans lived in foraging, or hunter-gatherer, societies that Marx called "primitive communism."‡ In most cases, these small cooperative communities had

* *Textile* means cloth or fabric. So why didn't I just say "cloth factories"? Because when you're writing about history, you're supposed to throw in some words that nobody says anymore. This is also how I'm justifying all my outdated Gen X cultural references.

† And there would be more crimes to come: child labor, colonialism, sweatshops, the Paul brothers...

‡ Marx meant *primitive* as in *early*, not *backward* or *simple-minded*, so it's

(and still have in a few cases) no classes or private property. Different foraging groups could wage war with one another (how often is a matter of debate), but it was also common for individuals to leave one group for another. Within a group, they shared resources because that's what made sense in societies in which everyone depended on one another for survival and happiness.

Foragers were nomads who consumed only as much food and clothing as they needed, in part because they had no permanent homes to keep large amounts of extra stuff. This kind of non-materialistic, non-hierarchical society sounded awful to the conservative English philosopher Thomas Hobbes, who famously argued that life in prehistoric societies that didn't have the benefit of rich and powerful kings must have been "nasty, brutish, and short." We now know that many of their lives were much longer than Hobbes supposed, and probably a lot less nasty than the lives of the poor in his England, which executed beggars for as little as stealing a few bird eggs.

Over thousands of years people learned how to domesticate plants and animals—in some places earlier than others—which gradually allowed them to produce more food than they needed and to store the surplus in case of future famine, which in turn led some people to stop being nomads and create settlements, which would eventually become towns and later civilizations. These developments, which are known together as the Neolithic Revolution, were both a historic advance and setback for humanity. They saved many from starvation during bad years and allowed for some people to be freed from daily toil to further develop our species' art, technology, and belief systems. But they also led to a more ominous innovation: the beginnings of a distinct ruling elite.

The specific features of class societies differed widely in various parts of the world. In some cases, respected members of the group who were tasked with deciding how to allocate the surplus grain evolved over generations into a permanent elite class. Other early ruling classes were violent oppressors from the start, taking advantage of the fact that farmers, unlike foragers, were tied to their land

---

not as bad as it sounds to modern ears. Not gonna lie though, it's a little sketchy.

and couldn't simply escape to a neighboring society. Whatever their origins, as elites became more removed from the rest of society over time, they created new traditions and institutions to make their dominance more permanent and secure. They developed a new category of property that was not communal but individually owned (or "private") to keep some of the surplus for themselves and the concept of personal inheritance to keep it within their families after they died.

The radical scholars David Graeber and David Wengrow argue that the development of agriculture didn't automatically lead to increasing hierarchy and class divisions. They note that modern research is uncovering more and more examples of ancient societies that bucked this trend—from egalitarian cities in Ukraine three thousand years ago to the possible democratization of the famous Mayan city of Teotihuacán in the year 300 AD.* This is obviously an exciting trend in archeology (a phrase I've never used before) that can help us see that human societies can evolve in different directions and that our course of development is not set in stone. Well, except for the artifacts at these excavation sites, which probably were in fact set in sto— You know what? We're going to move on from archeology.

Despite these inspiring counterexamples, many places in the world over time did see the combined emergence of agriculture, private property, and inheritance—as well as a fourth development that Friedrich Engels called "a world historic defeat for the female sex." The tradition of inheritance increased the importance of determining the parents of each child. Since it's usually pretty obvious during childbirth who the mother is, this led to women's sexual monogamy

* These and other examples are from Graeber and Wengrow's fascinating *The Dawn of Everything: A New History of Humanity*, which was annoyingly published just as I was trying to meet this book's deadline and not trying to rethink all my assumptions about the origins of civilization. I don't think the book proves all of its far-reaching claims, but it makes a powerful case that many notions of equality and democracy credited to the European Enlightenment may come from Native American ideas, and that these ideas, far from representing a "primitive stage" of humanity, were the result of centuries of political debates and upheavals.

being strictly enforced in a way it didn't have to be for men.* And so was born men's fears of being "cucked"—and their desire to control all aspects of female bodies and sexuality.

The onset of women's systematic oppression was also rooted in the fact that having many children is more useful in an agricultural society where they can be extra hands in the fields than it is in a hunter-gatherer society where they are mostly extra mouths to feed. Thus, women's lives became primarily about bearing, nursing, and raising children, which removed them from the authority of being breadwinners (bread-growers, really) in the fields. While women had played a central role in the leadership structures of most foraging societies, many agricultural societies excluded them from public leadership and introduced gender inequality alongside class inequality.

Gender oppression both inside the family and in public society has been central to all oppressive societies ever since. This might be one reason why many conservatives today get so personally threatened by transgender folks going to the bathroom, women having abortions, and lots of other stuff that should have nothing to do with them but has everything to do with maintaining an unjust social order.

Private property, inheritance, and women's subordination originated in the earliest ruling classes. The English word *family* comes from the Latin *familia*, a term that included everyone in a rich ancient Roman man's household, from wife and children to slaves and servants.† But over time these ruling-class structures became accepted norms for all members of most agricultural class societies—although of course the specific forms they took varied widely as human civilization spread and developed throughout the world. Over the past few thousand years many different types of societies came into being in which minority ruling classes have controlled the economic surplus created by the masses and put them to different uses. In the ancient eras of Athens, Mexico, and Mali, small segments of the populace

* If you're not sure why this is, ask the kids at school to draw you some pictures.

† Nice little fact to have in your pocket the next time your husband or father tells you to do the dishes. You're welcome.

living off the labor of conquered slaves built astounding legacies of science, art, and philosophy. The lands that today are Germany and Japan saw feudal societies in which each wealthy landowner used the food and crafts created by his peasants to pay for elaborate castles and warriors to raid other wealthy landowners' castles.

It was out of these types of feudal societies in Europe that capitalism began to develop, first through merchants and wealthy craftsmen, then through factory owners and bankers, and now through faceless international conglomerates and fame-seeking billionaires.* Capitalism is more productive and innovative—for good and evil—than previous class societies. That's because it is based not only on land but on capital that can be reinvested—as well as on competition between capitalists, which forces them to take most of the capital created by their workers and invest it back into developing new methods of creating even more capital. This is why technology has developed much more in one capitalist decade than it did for entire centuries before the 1800s.† It's also why the European and North American countries that developed capitalism first gained an enormous advantage that enabled them to drag the rest of the world into their new system on quite unfavorable terms.

Capitalism has achieved amazing things, some of which are appreciated most of all by socialists, who aren't hindered by the Social Darwinist nonsense about this being humanity's natural state. The first part of *The Communist Manifesto* has surprising praise of the capitalist class as "the first to show what man's activity can bring about. It has accomplished wonders far surpassing Egyptian pyramids, Roman aqueducts, and Gothic cathedrals." These wonders—from railroads to space flight—promise a future of widespread abundance and leisure time (that has been around the corner for the past two hundred years). Instead, railroads, built by legions of mostly

---

* Yes, crafts*men* and not crafts*people*. I never use *man* to refer to *people* and I apologize in advance for some people I quote in this book who do, as Marx is about to in a few paragraphs.

† The phenomenon of everybody over the age of thirty-five feeling hopelessly intimidated by the latest technology is a recent development. No farmer ever needed to ask his seven-year-old daughter how to work "this new-fangled steel plow thingy."

Chinese migrants, were used to wipe out Indigenous nations, while space travel devolved from scientific moon exploration to oligarchic penis compensation.

The problem is that while capitalism produces so much wealth that for the first time in history there is enough for many billions of people to live in abundance, it still relies on the (no longer true) assumption from earlier societies that there is a limited surplus that must be controlled and guarded by a small minority, forcing most of us to go to work for them and create more capital. In other words, capitalism has created a world in which capitalists should now be obsolete.

For almost all of our species' history, our main problem has been not having enough: not enough food, fertile land, or drinkable water. Now we produce too much, which should be a cause for celebration but instead is a curse, because when capitalists overproduce they lose on their investment and lay off millions of workers. Our second-biggest problem used to be disease. Today vaccines and treatments exist for the most widespread illnesses around the world, such as malaria and COVID, but their supply is limited to drive up the price beyond what many can afford and punish those living in countries that don't pledge allegiance to the flag of the United States of America.

But it's not only the poorest and most oppressed who experience the outmoded irrationality of capitalism. Anyone can do it! Just go online. The internet is the most important technological development of our time: a communication system in which information, ideas, and art are instantly shared and collaboratively developed across the world. It's so amazing that it's taken capitalism decades to figure out how to ruin it and make it something privately hoarded and sold. This process was relatively smooth for some traditional businesses that have simply shifted their focus to online sales, but many of the biggest internet sites are entirely based on content created and shared by users. Some, like Wikipedia and Craigslist, have embraced the non-capitalist model. But others like Google and Facebook spent years trying to figure out how to convert their usefulness into profit, until they finally found a way: by selling user information to advertisers who can now track our every online move.

Alongside the "law of the jungle," we now have the equally misleading metaphor of "the cloud," a gravity-free realm of limitless data and endless possibility, where government regulations would just harsh the heavenly vibe. In reality the cloud is millions of pounds of cables, cell towers, and servers that are owned by the most powerful monopolies in the world and designed to harvest our brains for as much data as possible. When I was a kid, the comedian Yakov Smirnoff did "Russian Reversal" jokes in a corny accent: "In America you can always find a party! In Soviet Russia, Party always find you!" Maybe somewhere today a comedian is working on her American Reversal routine: "In capitalist America, Google search you!"

What the Harvard business professor Shoshana Zuboff calls "surveillance capitalism" is a creepy web of control in which Facebook, Google, and the rest have us enveloped. It sounds like a villainous plot from a sci-fi movie.* But there was no sinister master plan—only capitalist investors searching for ways to make the internet worth their investment. If Mark Zuckerberg and Sergey Brin evolved from vaguely anti-establishment computer geeks into all-powerful dystopian ghouls, it wasn't due to some "law of nature" but capitalism's very un-Darwinian inability to adapt to the genuine sharing economy that the internet had potential to bring about.

It's time to take charge of our own evolution and have the majority who create society's wealth control how it is distributed. We now have the ability to combine the technology, wealth, and global communication of twenty-first-century capitalism with the egalitarianism and democracy of earlier societies, and realize an age-old dream of humanity. As Marx once put it, we can move beyond the realm of necessity into the realm of freedom.

---

* I'm talking about the Matrix, in which a digital reality keeps us unaware that we are literally being farmed by robots, but I'm embarrassed about making a second reference to the same movie in the main text. I feel more comfortable exposing my limited cultural literacy down here in the footnotes. Anyways, I highly recommend Zuboff's *The Age of Surveillance Capitalism* and *The Twittering Machine* by Richard Seymour.

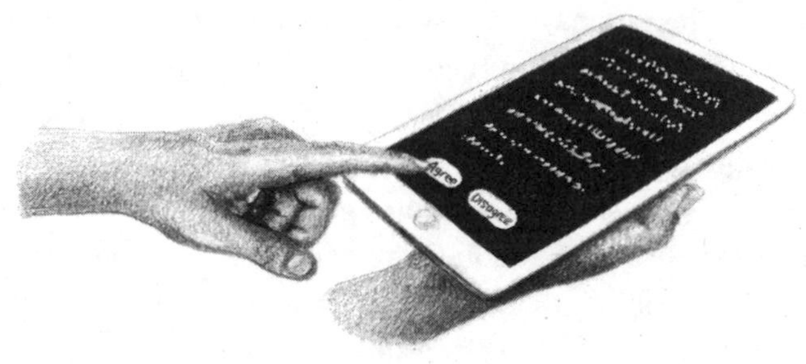
Agree
Disagree

4.

FREEDOM AND THE FINE PRINT

Socialism may be a good idea, but

... it doesn't work in practice.

... human beings are too greedy.

... the rich and powerful will never allow it.

You've probably heard one of these claims in school, online, around the dinner table. There even used to be a popular bumper sticker that went a step further than *good*: "Socialism . . . a Great Idea until You Run Out of Other People's Money." I realize the guy rocking this sticker alongside "Blue Lives Matter" and "Ax the Vax!" probably doesn't mean it as a compliment, but it's interesting that even hostile opponents of socialism often begin by admitting that it sure sounds nice.

The gist of this argument is that, for all its problems, capitalism is the only realistic form for society to take—whereas, as Homer Simpson once declared, "In theory, communism works—*in theory*." The second part of this book will consider if socialism is just a utopian fantasy, but now let's look at how capitalism works—*in theory*.

If there is a Karl Marx of capitalism, it's Adam Smith, the Scottish philosopher and economist who in 1776 wrote *The Wealth of Nations*, the book that introduced the world to the concepts of the "free market" and the "invisible hand." Smith meant these to be metaphors that could help people understand the complicated workings of this new social order he was trying to describe, but economists have instead treated them as not just real societal forces but demigods that must worshipped and appeased. But we shouldn't blame

Adam Smith for the stupidities of people who claim to be his disciples.* Before we get into the weaknesses in his theories, let's consider their positive contributions.

Smith didn't invent capitalism. He observed it from his perch as a university professor in Glasgow, a Scottish city at the heart of the Industrial Revolution. Just a few generations before, most people in Scotland were peasants who farmed their own land, turned over part of their crop to their local lord, and kept whatever was left to feed and clothe themselves. By Smith's time, economic activity was increasingly based on the trade among merchants and manufacturers. More people were spending their days producing one particular product and using their wages from this work to buy food and clothing produced by others. Ironically for someone known today for his embrace of cutthroat capitalism, one of the things Smith appreciated most about his changing society was how it brought all sorts of people together in a shared economic project. In a famous passage from *The Wealth of Nations*, he marvels at the collaborative nature of this new economy:

> The woolen coat, for example, which covers the day-labourer, as coarse and rough as it may appear, is the produce of the joint labour of a great multitude of workmen. The shepherd, the sorter of the wool, the wool-comber or carder, the dyer, the scribbler, the spinner, the weaver, the fuller, the dresser, with many others, must all join their different arts in order to complete even this homely production.
>
> How many merchants and carriers, besides, must have been employed in transporting the materials from some of those workmen to others who often live in a very distant part of the country!
>
> . . . how many ship-builders, sailors, sail-makers, rope-makers, must have been employed in order to bring together the different drugs made use of by the dyer, which often come from the remotest corners of the world! . . .
>
> [I]f we examine, I say, all these things, and consider what a variety of labour is employed about each of them, we shall be sensible that without the assistance and cooperation of many thou-

* The same is true for Marx, who disagreed so strongly with many of his followers that he once declared, "If anything is certain, it is that I myself am not a Marxist."

> sands, the very meanest person in a civilized country could not be provided, even according to, what we very falsely imagine, the easy and simple manner in which he is commonly accommodated.

Smith doesn't say whether the "remotest corners of the world" have been invaded and colonized, and if their materials are better described as stolen than traded. Notice also that he has chosen to detail the making of a garment made of wool rather than cotton—which would force him to talk about the not-so-cooperative form of labor known as slavery. Looking at this new system through Smith's eyes, however, reminds us that there is something awe-inspiring about the ways that capitalism has tied humanity together through millions of daily productive relationships. Marx and others would build on this part of Smith's vision. But we're not there yet. In 1776, the working class had barely begun to exist in a few cities like Glasgow. It would be another thirty years until it began taking large-scale strike actions and putting forward its own ideas about how the world should be run.

The people who grabbed Smith's attention were the capitalists, many of whom were his friends and neighbors. This rising new class was starting to amass great wealth, but it was not the capitalist class in power that we know today. At the time Britain was still mostly ruled by the aristocratic landowning class, with its rigid feudal hierarchies based on whether you were born into the family of the Duke of Dingleberry or the Earl of Flippybottom. In this context, *The Wealth of Nations* was a radical argument that the capitalist class had discovered a better way for society to be run.

This way was built upon three basic elements: self-interest, competition, and accumulation. Together these formed a potent synthesis. The first element drives innovation, the second spreads the benefits of innovation across society, and the third produces more innovation. Self-interest leads a capitalist to invest in manufacturing woolen coats to make a profit. Competition from other coat manufacturers ensures that the capitalist cannot charge an "unfair" price. This competition also leads the coat maker to not simply pocket his profits but to accumulate them to reinvest in better machinery and new technology to get ahead of the other manufacturers.

All of this activity takes place in what Smith called the free market, which is not a real place but a way to understand the commercial realm in which buyers and sellers trade goods and services. The key word for Smith was *free,* meaning that these are voluntary transactions. Unlike the obligatory relationships in previous societies between lords and peasants or slaves and slave owners, people can choose where to work, where to shop, and who to employ. Smith theorized that the free market is a self-regulating system for meeting society's needs that does not require (or benefit from) direction from any government. To explain this process, he used the image of an "invisible hand" that directs the millions of exchanges between buyers and sellers of goods and labor toward their most efficient and productive use for society.

Smith believed that capitalists' desire to make money and get ahead was a positive good for society, which has led many a modern executive to honor him as the patron saint of greed. But Smith was an intellectual, not a businessman—a champion of freedom and individual rights at a time when society's most cherished values were obedience and not challenging the destiny into which you were born. Smith's point was that the economic choices of millions of merchants, manufacturers, workers, and consumers would create a more intelligent society than the edicts of even the noblest king. His argument that an economy based on unregulated trade and competition was better than one rigidly controlled by the monarchy was in some ways a progressive case for democracy.

The next two centuries would prove him right. And also wildly wrong, since capitalism has led to more death and destruction than the most ruthless kings in history could ever have dreamed of causing: world wars, mass starvation, enslavement and forced migrations, and ecological devastation. Why did Smith's grand promises for capitalism flame out spectacularly in practice? Because far below the bold-type pronouncements about freedom are hundreds of pages of fine print indicating all the people, places, and hours of our days for which the rights to life, liberty, and the pursuit of happiness do not apply.

Tyranny: Exploitation, Oppression, and Theft

When the COVID pandemic forced the US government to increase unemployment benefits in 2020, millions of workers suddenly had an option to not go back to their lousy and poorly paying jobs. This might have been the most significant increase in American freedom since the legalization of same sex marriage. But instead of celebrating, our patriotic leaders complained about the new "labor shortage." Of course, there wasn't a shortage of workers but a drastic decline in the national supply of desperation.*

It was a moment of exposure for one of capitalism's dirty secrets: the decision to work for someone else—to sell our labor on the market—is only a voluntary or "free decision" for rich people who don't have to work in order to survive. The rest of us are forced to labor for others, just as the underclass majority has done for thousands of years. The only freedom that a worker has under capitalism—and it's a very important one—is that she doesn't have to toil for a particular lord or slave owner for the rest of her life but can bounce around working for many different bosses—sometimes by her choice and sometimes by theirs.

Freedom means different things to those standing on different sides of the checkout counter at the free market. For workers, guaranteed access to decent health care, housing, food, and transportation would give us more liberty to choose whether and when to sell our labor. But business owners denounce these ideas, along with minimum wage laws, unemployment insurance, and unions, for interfering with the magical workings of the Invisible Hand. Their real objection is that the more we are empowered to refuse dead-end and abusive jobs, the less freedom they have to pay and treat us however they want.

Capitalism would quickly cease to function if most people had the genuine freedom of economic security. Few people would work minimum-wage or highly dangerous jobs. In fact, few people would work for anybody else, period—because to work for someone else

* For some but not all. Undocumented workers were ineligible for most pandemic benefits, had to continue working in unsafe conditions, and suffered some of the highest death rates.

under capitalism is to be exploited. All bosses—not just the mean ones—exploit their workers, by which I mean all bosses keep for themselves some of the value produced by workers. This theft is how businesses make profits.

Let's say I own a company that makes vinyl records for a music label that specializes in mashups of German house music and 1990s New Jack Swing.* Not surprisingly, we're a very small business with only one employee: you. You make $25 an hour, or $200 for an eight-hour day. Each day we make (okay, you make) fifty LPs of *Bell Biv DeVolkswagen* that sell for $10 each, for a total of $500. (For the purposes of this example, we'll assume that every record will be sold, although that's not how it works in the real world, as we'll get to later.) As a worker, you spend your days listening to Tony! Toni! Toné! Teutonic techno mashups, acutely aware that you are receiving $25 for every hour that you don't run screaming out of the building.

As the owner, I look at your day quite differently. My daily expenses are $200 for your salary plus another $200 for rent, machinery, and other materials. From my perspective, the first twenty LPs you make—which take you a little over three hours—pay off your wages. The next twenty pay for my other expenses. Now that I've made my $400 back, the final part of your day when you make the last ten LPs belongs completely to me. I keep that final $100 as a profit on my $400 investment. Whether or not you're happy to be making $25 an hour, I have kept for myself some of the wealth that you created. If the business grows and I have ten employees, I'll be making $1,000 a day, "earning" that profit not by making the LPs—and certainly not by providing the world with good music—but simply because I had the capital in the first place to rent the space and buy the materials. And chances are, the reason you are the one doing the work and not seeing the profit is because you didn't.

This relationship between those who are forced to sell their labor and those who have the capital to buy that labor and use it to make a profit is what socialists call exploitation. All profits are based on

* Obviously, this is just a humorous hypothetical—unless you think this could work, in which case contact me ASAP.

exploitation, which is obvious to anyone who has ever had a job, but also tricky to prove. In the daily workings of capitalism, a company's profitability can depend on many changing factors, from the price of raw materials to current consumer tastes.

This is supposed to be why we have a science called economics. Science is good at explaining things that we can't figure out through everyday experience, like germs and evolution. Unfortunately, most of what we know as economics isn't based on objective research on how capitalism works but propaganda promoting its wonders.

You might think, for example, that economics textbooks would be interested in understanding the source of profits. After all, profit is the first consideration in almost every major decision our society makes. The hunt for profit is why we are bombarded every year with meaningless new versions of toothpaste, and it's also why seventy-five million Americans are denied dental insurance and can't go to the dentist. Your daughter's school has replaced art, music, and gym with more standardized tests because politicians hope this will one day make her a more profit-generating worker, and your father's old factory has been moved a thousand miles to a lower-wage area so that his company can make even more profits.

And yet most textbooks don't even devote a single chapter to the question of where profit comes from. They simply take its existence for granted and move right on to supply and demand, efficiency and elasticity, and other factors that explain what makes profits rise and fall. This may be all that matters from the perspective of capitalists, but it doesn't answer the question of what makes the total amount of society's capital grow larger, as it does every year except during recessions. In effect, mainstream economics deals with profits the way any of us would regard a bank account that mysteriously gained an extra thousand dollars each month that we couldn't account for. We would certainly think a lot about what to do with that extra money, but we wouldn't ask too many questions about where it came from, suspecting that we probably don't want to know the answer.

When the question of profits is addressed in mainstream economics, it's not to figure out where they came from but to justify why they should go to bosses who often did little to earn them. Thus, many economists claim that profits are a reward given to capitalists for the risk of investing in a business. Somehow, according to this theory, the Invisible Hand actually belongs to a jolly Invisible Uncle who likes to slip a little something extra to bosses as a show of gratitude for their bravery. The most laughable part is the idea that it's rich people who are the major risk-takers in our society. If capitalism really awarded profits to those who took risks to add to the national wealth, bosses and investors would have to get far back in line behind firefighters, miners, and undocumented construction workers.

Defenders of capitalism reach for these and other outlandish theories because it's awkward to acknowledge that the real source of profit is the workers who don't see any of it. But if you're not in the business of apologizing for the system, you can actually recognize that there is some good news here. We are an intelligent and creative species that has figured out how to produce far more than we need to personally consume. This productivity, if allocated fairly and rationally, would be fantastic news: no more hunger and homelessness, no need to pollute the planet, and no coming back to work after lunch!

But no, under capitalism workers don't get to decide what to do with the surplus they create. Instead that money goes into profits, which owners use partly on nice suits and luxury homes but mostly plow back into production—often to exploit us more or even replace us. Technological advancements that we are promised will make our jobs easier are used to make us work harder. That incredible new software program that you thought would save you some time entering data is now causing the person in the next cubicle to be laid off—and you're expected to pick up half their work.

Many workers are not exploited in the strict economic sense of the word because they don't work for a private company, but they have a similar relationship to capitalism. Government employees such as teachers, mail carriers, and highway workers have salaries that come from taxes paid by the entire population. But the decisions about how, where, and for how much they do their jobs are still determined by the needs of business—specifically its desire to spend the least amount of tax dollars required to have an adequately educated labor force that can make it to work on time. Protests for more funding for schools and post offices are therefore fights over the use of capitalists' profits, just as much as strikes in corporate-owned factories.

Then there are the millions of people, primarily women, who don't get paid a dime for the countless hours spent caring for children, parents, and other family members. They often don't even think of themselves as exploited workers because these vital activities aren't viewed as "real" work, but their labor saves capitalism untold amounts of money in feeding, clothing, and educating its workforce. The global charity Oxfam estimates the global annual value of women's unpaid work to be at least $10.8 trillion—three times larger than the world's tech industry.

All told, workers make up the majority of people, which is a potential problem for bosses who depend on their labor to keep generating profits. In the early 1800s the poet Percy Shelley wrote these inspiring lines:

Rise, like lions after slumber
In unvanquishable number—
Shake your chains to earth like dew
Which in sleep had fallen on you—
Ye are many—they are few!

Today *ye* are many more than *ye* were in Shelley's day, while *they* are still pretty few. In order to avoid getting overthrown by a mob of unvanquishable lions, much less keep us at our jobs every day making their profits, capitalists need ways to keep us in our place. This is where oppression comes in. Oppression refers to the systemic mistreatment of some group of people on the basis of their race, gender, disability, sexual identity, or some other factor. It both weakens specific groups of people and keeps them divided from others with whom they could potentially unite.

Note the word *systemic*—as in something rooted in societal institutions, not unpleasant individual interactions. Men are not oppressed by women, no matter how many angst-ridden songs they write about having their hearts broken. Sexism, racism, and other oppressions are often thought of as individual prejudices—stupid or mean ideas passed down from one generation to the next. This often shifts the focus onto ordinary people—especially poor and working-class ones who don't go to private schools and universities that train them to subtly disguise their prejudice. But oppression comes straight from the top of society. It's about some people getting worse educations, job and housing opportunities, and health care than others, and being made to feel through advertising, schools, and interactions with police and other authorities that they are second-class citizens.

That's why most corporate statements against oppression often ring hollow, even if they may be sincere and well intentioned. I live near a Starbucks with a sign in the window that proudly proclaims the store a space where racism and sexism won't be tolerated. I hope the sign makes people feel a little more welcome, but it can't address the fact that inside the store there are mostly Black and brown female employees being exploited for the profits going to the company's mainly white male executives and shareholders.

There's a complicated relationship between exploitation and oppression, and a lot can be learned from analyzing the interactions between race, class, and gender—as long as we keep in mind that that's exactly what it is: an interaction. Exploitation and oppression are not rivals but partners. It's impossible to imagine the exploitation of African Americans through slavery and sharecropping without the racism that held them to be subhuman, just as there is no way that women could be paid less than their male counterparts without a sexist framework that they should be expected to prioritize family over work. The oppression of people with disabilities allows employers to get away with not spending some of their profits on creating accessible workplaces, while the oppression of Indigenous people enables companies to illegally build mines and pipelines on lands that should be protected by treaties.

One group whose oppression is often not talked about is the working class—of all races and genders. Workers go to inferior schools, receive substandard health care, and are often treated with contempt by societal institutions. When workers protest or strike, they can be handled roughly by the police and courts in ways that would never fly for those in the middle or upper classes. But the core of workers' oppression takes place, unsurprisingly, at work, where many laws simply don't apply. An Amazon worker has about as much right to freedom of speech when she's on "company time" as a peasant did on the lord's property. Legally binding contracts with workers—such as pension agreements—are somehow less legally binding than contracts with banks, such as loans. Sexual harassment, racial discrimination, bullying, and abuse are all standard habits of many successful managers. It's because the workplace operates so differently from any conceivable notion of freedom that capitalism encourages us to think of ourselves as consumers rather than workers—even though most of us spend far more time working than we do shopping.

But oppression is also an entirely separate thing from exploitation, with very different characteristics. Not only that, but each form of oppression has its own unique features and history that have to be understood on their own. Indigenous people, for example, face constant erasure and denial of their existence as part of the centuries-long project of hiding their rightful claim to this continent. African Americans, on the other hand, deal with the entirely different plight of relentless demonization and hyper-scrutiny as this country's eternal scapegoat.

Exploitation remains a constant fact of capitalism, but oppressions can rise and fall in intensity. The oppression of women, as we have seen, has existed for thousands of years, while the oppression of ethnic groups like the Italians and Irish in the United States only lasted a couple of generations. The persecution of Muslims in the US and around the world has grown horribly worse over the "War on Terror" decades. That's the same era in which cultural shifts and activism have led to real gains for many LGBTQ people—although I'm writing this at a moment when horrific anti-trans laws are being pushed across Republican-led states.

The uniqueness of each type of oppression makes it an effective tool for dividing people and getting them to buy into one another's oppressions even as they suffer their own. It's also true, however, that people's shared experience of some sort of oppression can be a powerful basis for coming together, which is one reason why many social movements of the past decade have been shaped and led by trans and queer women of color. But that's a subject for the next section. We're still in the gloomy part of the book.

The point here is that the much-hyped freedoms of capitalism are mostly limited to a tiny minority that has the resources to make truly free choices. Emperors and slave owners from centuries past would not be totally unfamiliar with this variety of freedom.

Yet even the richest straight white men are not immune to capitalism's destructive ways. It's not only enraging to watch the richest people in the world squander billions of dollars on their fantasies of creating space colonies to leave the rest of us on a dying planet; it's pathetic that they think they can rich-guy their way out of this. I have similar feelings watching politicians lie about their plans to stop global burning, fooling themselves that they can bullshit nature the way they bullshit us. Rising oceans don't care about their bogus emissions pledges that they have no plans to enforce. Forest infernos are unimpressed by oil companies moving operations from Europe to Africa to give their home countries a cleaner-looking environmental record.

Many humans around the world aren't moved either. How are delegates in climate negotiations supposed to trust the word of countries with long histories of stealing land and breaking treaties? There may be honor among thieves, but not among imperialists. Conservatives sometimes talk about how an "ownership society" leads to greater personal and community responsibility. Besides being an elitist idea that could only come from people who have never been renters, it can't explain why those who own most of this country's land treat it so irresponsibly. That's where it's important to remember that the property some consider to be owned others know to have been taken. The US environment record reflects not a virtuous ownership society but what some Indigenous revolutionaries call a "live on it like you stole it" culture—the dangerous and seductive dream that if you turn your home into trash, you can just go west, take someone else's, and start over.*

* That's from *The Red Deal: Indigenous Action to Save Our Earth,* put out by the Red Nation.

Adam Smith's theories about free markets and invisible hands gained popularity in 1800s England with precisely the same people who boasted about having stolen so much of other people's land around the world that "the sun never sets on the British Empire." That era of open and proud colonialism is over (mostly), not because capitalist elites grew more enlightened but because their asses were kicked out of Africa, Asia, and Latin America by resistance movements led by people like Mahatma Gandhi, Kwame Nkrumah, and Ho Chi Minh. But capitalists in the wealthy countries have found more indirect methods, like offering loans and private investment in poor countries that were never compensated for being impoverished under colonialism—in return for the right to pay dirt poor wages and trash the local ecology.

The theft of other people's land and labor have long gone together. For thousands of years in much of Europe, Asia, and Africa, the conquest of a territory brought not only land but the forced labor of the people who lived there. But capitalism has a different relationship between land and labor. People need to be removed from their land and they are forced to sell their labor in factories—sometimes on the same land that was once theirs. This process was started with the English "enclosures" from the 1600s to 1800s, when rich lords eager to meet the growing demand for wool got the Parliament to fence off lands that used to be shared by the people as "commons" and turn them into privately owned grazing lands for the lords' sheep.

The enclosures devastated the rural poor, forcing them to migrate to the factories of the new Industrial Revolution, and turning sheep into an object of ridicule by conspiracy theorists for centuries to come.* Enclosures also contributed to a fundamental change in how people started viewing land. Under capitalism, land could be a source of increasing wealth not just by having more of it but by using it for more value-producing purposes, whether that was grazing sheep in 1650, growing cotton with enslaved labor in 1850, or tearing down affordable housing to

* I don't actually think "wake up sheeple!" comes from the British Enclosure Acts. But you can bet that if hucksters like Alex Jones were around back then, they would have riled up anger against the sheep instead of the landlords.

build luxury towers in 2020. This is the idea of land "improvement" that drove European claims to Indigenous territory. The issue wasn't that Native inhabitants hadn't greatly and sustainably enhanced their environment but that they weren't making money from it.*

By separating labor from land, capitalism figured out how to more efficiently exploit both. For hundreds of years, the capitalist approach of maximizing what could be extracted from both humans and nature worked spectacularly well for a minority of the world's population. But this accelerated exploitation has exhausted the soil, poisoned the rivers, overheated the atmosphere, and melted the poles. Plant and animal species are estimated to be going extinct anywhere from a thousand to ten thousand times the normal rate. It's the most horrifying proof that capitalism's fancy theories have failed miserably in the real world.

Anarchy: Competition and Crisis

I'll never forget the *New York Times* coverage of a 2012 announcement that the United States would soon surpass Saudi Arabia as the world's leading oil producer. The statement was described as "good news for the United States," but "more sobering for the planet"—as if both could be true at the same time. Eight years before Donald Trump's election, the *Times* seemed to think we could build a border fence high enough to block out rising levels of carbon dioxide.

The people running this country aren't really this dumb, with some occasional obvious exceptions. The problem is that as powerful as they are compared with us, they are not the true masters of society. Capitalism is run not by capitalists but by capital itself. My favorite description of this relationship comes from Thomas Dunning, an

* There are many darkly funny journal entries from European explorers amazed at the beautifully tended trails and pasturelands they "discovered" in the Americas. Rather than draw the obvious conclusion that these landscapes were being skillfully cultivated by Indigenous people they viewed as ignorant savages, these Godly killers would instead take it as divine approval that untouched wilds just happened to be so strangely prepared for immediate Christian settlement.

English worker and union organizer whose words were quoted in Marx's masterwork, *Capital*:

> Capital eschews no profit, or very small profit, just as Nature was formerly said to abhor a vacuum. With adequate profit, capital is very bold. A certain 10 percent will ensure its employment anywhere; 20 percent certain will produce eagerness; 50 percent, positive audacity; 100 percent will make it ready to trample on all human laws; 300 percent, and there is not a crime at which it will scruple, nor a risk it will not run, even to the chance of its owner being hanged.

If it seems I'm making capital sound like some mysterious evil force that gets inside people's heads like Sauron in *Lord of the Rings*, that's because I am.* Only I prefer *The Fifth Element*, where you can tell someone has been taken over by "The Great Evil" when a thick ooze (which happens to look like crude oil) starts to run down his forehead.† A bit over the top? Possibly, but when I think about fossil fuel executives pressuring governments to let them build more pipelines and sink more wells, even as they know that they might be sealing the planet's fate, I can't help but imagine black liquid slowly trickling down from their thousand-dollar haircuts.

When the ooze of capital enters a capitalist's brain, the main emotion that it manipulates is not greed—although there's plenty of that too—but fear. Capitalists are driven by the fear that if they don't increase profits, someone else will who could eventually put them out of business. Here is the second great flaw of Adam Smith's understanding of capitalism. Blind competition between capitalists really does produce an Invisible Hand of sorts, but this hand can destroy just as easily as it can create. A society that rewards selfishness and punishes sharing does not work very well even for some of those at the top of the capitalist food chain—and it's a disaster for the rest of

---

* Let Adam Smith have his free market and Invisible Hand. I'll take the description of bosses clutching profit reports and hissing, "Yessss, my precious."

† At this point you might uneasily be wondering if these 1990s references will continue for the whole book. To which I say, "Boo-yah!"

us. Far from being a reflection of human nature, pure individualism is violently alien to the human experience. We have always depended upon one another, as well as other species, for survival and happiness.

The failure of blind competition is just as evident economically as it is ecologically. Capitalists don't automatically profit from exploiting their workers. The product has to be sold in order to make a return on their investment, which means it's important to not produce too much. But overproduction is just what inevitably occurs in any profitable industry, not because individual capitalists can't control themselves but because they can't control their competition. If one company is making a killing on smartphones, other companies will jump in the market, and then others, until there are many more smartphones being made than people willing and able to buy them. The problem is exacerbated by the drive to pay workers as little as possible, which leads to most consumers not having enough money to buy all the extra crap created by capitalism.

The system has developed different ways to get around this contradiction: consumers and businesses are allowed to go deep into debt to keep buying products with money they don't really have; companies merge and buy one another out to form monopolies that reduce competition; apps on our phones spy on us so that businesses can maximize their advertising spending by finding the exact target audience for their products. All of it makes society worse and none of it solves the underlying problem. Eventually, the bills come due, consumers stop buying, companies start laying off workers, who themselves stop buying, and the economy goes into a downward spiral known as a recession.

Engels wrote that capitalism combines the tyranny of each boss over his workers with the anarchy of all the bosses' blind competition with one another on the market.* This has been a regular feature of capitalism since its inception. Economics textbooks feature lots

* Engels didn't mean *anarchy* as in the political ideal of a society without government but rather the other definition of the word that means a state of chaos and disorder. Many anarchists don't seem to mind this confusion, which I find both charming and unwise.

of charts showing a perfect harmony of supply and demand, but the real thing has instead been a wild ride of booms and recessions that even the most powerful industrialists have been unable to predict, much less control—although most of them are able to get through the stormy times okay by tossing some of us overboard. At times there are attempts to lessen the impact of recessions—like the expanded unemployment insurance during COVID—which can provide crucial relief but don't address the underlying crisis of a system that demands endless expansion from a world that can't endlessly expand.

Every recession brings about the ironic combination of empty foreclosed houses and abandoned shuttered factories with increased rates of homelessness and unemployment. Many of us have become so accustomed to capital's way of seeing the world that this doesn't strike us as immoral and illogical. Capitalism imposes the alien values of capital on human beings. Education is transformed from the ability to think for ourselves about the world around us into test results measuring the basic literacy and ability to sit still necessary to be good future employees. Neighborhoods are no longer communities of people who look after one another, but sets of property values that homeowners hope will keep rising even if gentrification forces out people they've known for decades.

In recent years, the Supreme Court has helpfully spelled out for anyone who didn't already know it that humans are second-class citizens in a world run by capital. The 2010 *Citizens United v. FEC* ruling infamously declared that "corporations are people." Among other things, this ruling has enabled businesses the "freedom of religion" to deny employees birth control coverage in their health care plans. While the court has granted corporations the rights of people, it has restricted the rights of actual human beings to protest in many locations or be protected from being detained by police without cause. The fanatics who currently make up a majority of the court would like to use the "find . . . replace" function on the entire Constitution, substituting *corporation* any time there is mention of *people* having rights.

(The origin story of the bizarre "corporations are people" idea is so wild, by the way, and involves a man with such a silly name, that it requires a brief tangent. Roscoe Conkling was a Congressman during the creation of the 14th Amendment, which guaranteed citizenship to all people born in the country. Fifteen years later Conkling had moved on to become a railroad company lawyer, and he now claimed that this amendment, meant to enfranchise Black people after the Civil War, was also meant to apply to . . . railroad companies. The court ignored this nonsense in his case, but over time conservative judges started falsely citing Conkling's claim as legal precedent and they kept at it for decades until people believed it. I swear this is the actual and only "legal precedent" for *Citizens United*. It should be taught in schools as the Conkling Theorum: *Lies + Time + More Lies = The Law.*[*])

It isn't just in the United States that capital outranks humans. Capital is a global citizen, able to move freely across borders, even as country after country builds walls and cracks down on people who try to do the same. What Adam Smith brilliantly understood was that capitalism created a world of freedom. The part he got wrong was that the citizens of this world would not be people but capital, a parasite that uses humanity as a host body to multiply itself even as it weakens our own natural instincts for love, compassion, and possibly even self-preservation.

---

* Historian Adam Winkler tells the story in *We the Corporations.*

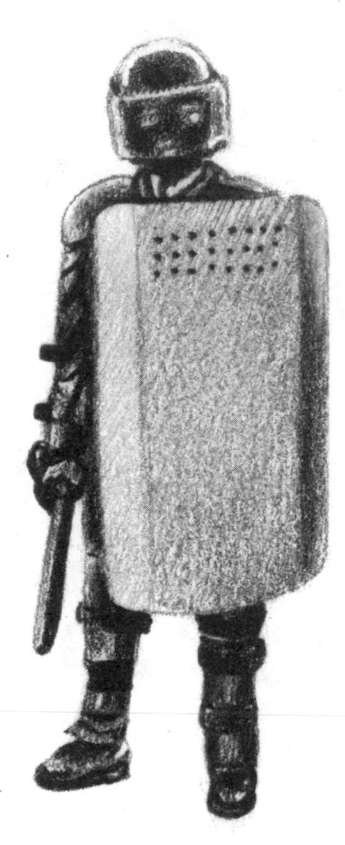

5.

THE DEEP STATE

As children, we are told a story: Once upon a time there was a dashing young economic system named Capitalism. Then one day, Capitalism met Democracy, the fairest political system of them all, and together they lived happily ever after. It's a great fairy tale, but the real Prince Capitalism isn't a noble suitor but a sleazy banker bro who will shack up with any political systems he meets—whether parliamentary democracies or military dictatorships or whatever that thing is in Washington, DC, where the people with bad tans and fake hair yell at each other for the cameras.

There is no inherent connection between capitalism and democracy. The great voting assemblies of ancient Athens didn't know anything about the profit system, while Hitler's fascist regime was great for Coca-Cola, IBM, and Ford.* In fact, full democracy is impossible under an economic system that depends on our lack of options. Capitalism, as we've discussed, allows us to choose what to buy and sell in the marketplace, but it also depends upon a few people owning most of the capital so that the rest of us have no choice over whether or not we want to sell our labor. A system like this simply cannot allow the majority of people to vote on whether or not this setup should be changed.

Instead, capitalist democracies grant us the right to vote, but about what, exactly? Can we democratically decide whether a company

* Henry Ford was such a notorious anti-Semite, it's a miracle he never went with the ad slogan, "Once you step into a Ford, you will NAZI yourself driving anything else!!"

should lay off its workers? No. Do we have a say over whether that company can at least not give its executives bonuses while laying off workers? No. Okay, fine. That's private enterprise. Can we vote on whether our government can spy on us? No.

In 2013, Edward Snowden blew the whistle on the vast domestic surveillance system of the National Security Agency (NSA). In one of his more patronizing moments, then-president Barack Obama responded not with an apology but a lecture. "You can't have 100 percent security and also then have 100 percent privacy and zero inconvenience," he said. "We're going have to make some choices as a society."

Who exactly did Obama mean by "we"? Did he actually mean all Americans? Would there be a series of public forums in every community debating the powers of the national security state? Or did the president's "we" refer to private negotiations between generals and tech company executives? The answer to that question tells us who makes the real decisions under capitalism.*

Your democratic rights can be further restricted if you're careless enough to live in a country not favored by the US empire. In 1983, the US invaded the Caribbean nation of Grenada because its government was building a desperately needed new airport, which then-president Ronald Reagan believed could be used by Russian communists on their way to Cuba. In 2006, Palestinians voted for the Hamas party to replace their corrupt incumbent government, but Israel and America declared the victors a terrorist organization who wouldn't be allowed to take office outside the tiny Gaza Strip.†

Even inside the US, many of us are denied our democratic rights. In its 2013 *Shelby County v. Holder* decision, the Supreme Court undermined the Voting Rights Act, using logic as clear as a broken

---

* In olden times, kings and queens used something called the "royal we." Obama invented a new pronoun: the "military-industrial-complex we."

† These days the first example is more widely condemned than the second. That's because it happened twenty years earlier, and just shouting "Communism!" no longer has the same mind-melting power that "Terrorism!" unfortunately retains.

mirror. The law is no longer needed to protect Black people's right to vote, the court ruled, because Black people were no longer in danger of not being allowed to vote, because the Voting Rights Act protected Black people's right to vote. It was the legal equivalent of a hospital removing your pacemaker because your heart was doing much better ever since they put in the pacemaker, and somewhere in hell Roscoe Conkling was no doubt smiling.

On top of the suppression of legal voters is the more old-fashioned method of denying the franchise to poor and nonwhite people. The number of Americans barred from voting because they are not citizens or because they are currently or formerly incarcerated is almost 10 percent of the voting-age population.* That's more than the margin of victory in most presidential elections.

For those of us allowed to vote, local elections are often symbolic affairs in which everyone already knows who's going to win. Thanks to gerrymandering, the process where the voting district boundaries are drawn up to deliberately include a majority of Democratic or Republican voters, nine out of ten members of Congress enjoy "non-competitive" elections where the other party has no chance of defeating them. As a result, the most competitive non-presidential elections take place inside party primaries, where public attention and voter turnout is far lower. Socialists in recent years have managed to figure out how to play this rigged game and win some historic elections but then face the challenge of operating inside a system that discourages the mass participation and protest needed to win the groundbreaking policies they got elected to pass.

Which brings us to the final step of how not to have a vibrant democracy: a two-party system in which the progressive option is one of the more racist and violent organizations in modern world history. Yes, I'm talking about the Democratic Party, and if you think I'm exaggerating, consider that their track record includes:

---

* Another consequence of the US locking up more of its people than any other country is that more than a third of US adults face some form of legal discrimination either because they have a criminal record or because they are undocumented.

- The "Trail of Tears"
- The invasion of Mexico
- The Civil War—on the slavery side!
- Jim Crow segregation
- Dropping nuclear bombs on the people of Hiroshima and Nagasaki
- Killing many millions in senseless wars in Korea and Vietnam
- Mass incarceration in the 1990s and mass deportations in the 2000s

I'll admit that this is a biased list intended to make the party look bad, and that I could have included the good things Democrats have done (under extreme pressure from protest movements) such as the Social Security and the Civil Rights Acts. That's my bad. I have this problem sometimes where I don't feel enough gratitude because I'm dwelling on the mass murder.

Aren't the Republicans even worse? For most of their history, absolutely.* But that's my point. Both major US parties are devoted to the priorities of the tiny class that runs this country, with the important but still small exception of the new socialist wing inside the Democrats. Of course, they are not the same—if they were, it would be a one-party system. Democrats fight for us to have the worst health care system among wealthy nations, while Republicans want it to be even worse than that.

Most of the people who vote for Democrats, on the other hand, are far more progressive, which means the two parties have very different ways of getting their supporters to accept the same outcomes. Republicans drain government budgets to give billionaires more tax breaks and proudly declare they are weaning us off our dangerous addiction to public services like schools and hospitals. Democrats angrily promise to undo the damage, but whenever they get the chance there are a few who change their minds—and by some strange coincidence there

* The Republicans began as a third party opposed to the expansion of slavery, which is why they like to call themselves "the party of Lincoln." But barely a decade after the Civil War they started to become the slimeballs we know today. (See: Conkling, Roscoe)

are always just enough of them to stop the Democrats from having a majority to fulfill their promises. Some Democrats, perhaps many, are sincerely progressive. But they are members of a party that is the loud guy in the bar pretending to be held back by his friends to keep him from going after someone he has absolutely no intention of fighting.

Billionaires or Democracy

People who are frustrated with the two-party system frequently talk about the government being broken. But the government works well enough for the One Percent, whose tax breaks still get done on time. And even when Congress is unable to pass any legislation, the government manages to bomb rural villages, tear away asylum-seeking children from their parents, and approve new oil drilling permits. The only broken part of the government is the relatively small section with the people we are allowed to elect. That's because it's impossible to have a society with vast economic inequality that does not also have vast political inequality. Here's another way to put it: you can have billionaires or you can have democracy, but you cannot have a lot of both.

To understand why, we first have to wrap our heads around just how much a billion dollars is, because unless you are a billionaire—and that is not the target demographic of this book—I guarantee you don't get it. We tend to use the word *billion* to refer to some countless number just shy of infinity, a ludicrous exaggeration of a million not much different than fake numbers like *bajillion* and *shlazillion.** A billion is an actual number—a thousand millions, to be precise. But it is a ludicrous amount of money for one person to own.

The typical family in the United States (forget most of the world) had about $120,000 in net worth, as of 2019. If that all-American family were to stack its wealth in 120,000 individual dollar bills lined end to end, it would extend over eleven miles in the air. "Son, that's twice as tall as Mount Everest," Dad might proudly say as he takes a satisfied

* Nobody actually says *shlazillion*, but I'm trying to make that a thing—as in "There were a shlazillion people at that protest!" or "*Socialism . . . Seriously* is selling shlazzy copies, yo." Help me out: #shlazillion

puff on his pipe and Sparky gives a bark of approval.* But a billion is more than eight thousand times larger than 120,000, so if Facebook founder Mark Zuckerberg showed up and did the same thing, his $97 billion in wealth would stretch all the way to the moon... and back... thirty-five times.

Back on Earth, vast discrepancies in wealth lead to vast discrepancies in power—over all of us. Most readers of this book could probably use an extra eight thousand dollars: to pay off debt, put something away for retirement, or even take a real-life vacation. Imagine what unpleasant, embarrassing, or even immoral tasks you might agree to do in exchange for eight thousand dollars.... Okay, stop imagining. That was disgusting.

Here's my point: since a billion dollars is eight thousand times what the average American owns, a billionaire could get you to do that thing for eight thousand dollars, and for him it would be like throwing you a single. For a thousand billionaire dollars, he could debase not just you but our entire political system, because that's $8 million in regular people money—enough to fund a think tank, hire a click farm, and buy off some Congresspeople to promote whatever twisted ideas he wants. Having a billion dollars endows him with godlike powers, and the number of billionaires in the United States has risen from thirteen in 1982 to more than seven hundred today. We are seeing the rise of a new race of supermen, and they're not the good guys.

This isn't about petty jealousy. That money came from us! The growing wealth of the superrich coincides with declining wealth for the rest of us—not just our personal savings, but the collective wealth of our schools and post offices, our job security and health benefits, and expectations that our kids will have it better than we do. Economic inequality inevitably leads to political inequality, and just as the rich have been gaining political power, we have been losing it. We aren't just poorer; we're sicker and less organized. We work longer hours, pay more for health care, scramble to deal with more precarious child-care arrangements. We face more repression from law enforcement

* There is no dog, by the way, just a fourteen-year-old boy named Sparky who is going through a phase. Sorry if that wasn't clear.

when we try to protest—or, if we are immigrants, Muslims, or African Americans, even when we don't.

Democracy is an ancient Greek word that means "rule by the people" and how democratic any society should be judged is based on not only its formal political structures but on the capacity that its people are granted to genuinely rule in their own interest. In his dense but fascinating four-book series called *Karl Marx's Theory of Revolution*, Hal Draper tells us that the word *democracy* was just coming back into popular use in Marx's day, after being buried for two thousand years by horrified European ruling classes, and that it could have multiple meanings. In addition to referring to a political system based on elections and individual liberties, democracy could also refer to mass movements or even popular sentiment. The nineteenth-century Chartist movement in England, the first mass movement of the modern working class, referred to itself as *the democracy*.

There is an echo of this older usage today in the popular protest chant: *This is what democracy looks like!* For the most part, however, our definition—and understanding—of democracy has become unfortunately limited to a set of laws. Socialists retain the older, more multifaceted definition because it makes it clear that democracy is something that has to be constantly fought for, even when we live in a political system that calls itself a democracy.

Abolish the Real "Deep State"

Every state hides its unaccountable authority by claiming to be so connected to us that accountability is unnecessary. The US government refers to itself in court cases as "The People" just as China calls itself the "People's Republic." This isn't a new development. Frederick the Great of Prussia justified his monarchy by claiming that "the prince is to the nation he governs what the head is to the man; it is his duty to see, think, and act for the whole community."

In truth the first role of states has always been to see, think, and act for the ruling classes of their time, be they slave owners, feudal aristocrats, or transnational corporations. Marx and Engels wrote in

The Communist Manifesto that the role of capitalist states was to be "a committee for managing the common affairs of the whole bourgeoisie."* This is a vital function because capitalists are too blinded by competition in pursuit of immediate profits to engage in long-term planning. Capitalists are like children, and it's the state's job to be the grown-up pushing the shopping cart while capitalists sit in the front and make a grab for whatever they want, leaving the state to clean up their spills and put the five boxes of Frosted Flakes back on the shelf.

Capitalists need the state not just to babysit them but to create the basic conditions that make profitable investment possible. Just as the profit system in England depended on enclosure laws to overturn the long tradition of common land, in the United States it depended on military force to dispossess Native peoples of their commons—and then a legal system crafted to spin that theft into law. The Supreme Court's earliest rulings also established that business contracts and private property were more important than democracy. In the 1810 case of *Fletcher v. Peck*, for example, the court ruled that the Georgia legislature could not overturn a (stolen Indigenous) land deal that had been passed by previous lawmakers—even though it turned out almost all of them had been bribed to pass the deal! This principle that punishing business crimes is less important than creating a stable investment climate has been the law—or lack of law—of the land ever since.

Modern governments are vast and complex organizations with thousands of functions, so it would be silly to see public employees as tools of capitalist repression. The state is responsible for many vital services that should be expanded and improved, from monitoring public health to providing free education, disability benefits, and mail delivery. It also plays many other roles that socialists aim to reduce

---

* *Bourgeoisie* is a French word that means middle class, but it is also the term Marx and others used for the capitalist class, because it originated as a class in between the peasants and the aristocracy. Just to be clear, this is different from what people mean today by *bougie*. Marx wasn't saying that getting an extra sprinkle of cinnamon in your latte made you a member of the ruling elite.

and eliminate, such as throwing people in jail and chasing down migrants who cross national borders. Black socialists like Angela Davis and Ruth Wilson Gilmore have spent decades organizing around the idea of defunding and abolishing the side of government that oppress people and putting those resources into the side that supports them. When their abolitionist ideas gained ground during the Black-led rebellion of 2020, they were treated as absurdly radical by establishment figures. But for decades conservatives have waged an abolitionist movement against the good side of government. This movement has successfully defunded schools, libraries, and mental health supports in the name of fighting the tyranny of "Big Government," while throwing ever more money at the actual forces of state tyranny: the military, police, prison, border patrol, and spy agencies.

This is an old story. The American Revolution was led by wealthy white colonists—many of them enslavers—who were outraged at having to pay more taxes even as they hypocritically demanded more military support from England to drive off Indigenous people in the Ohio Valley. They wrote a constitution that reflected the contradictory desires for a big government military and a small government to keep its nose out of the affairs of Southern slave plantations.* And up through today there is a strong American tradition of loudly complaining about "welfare" and "entitlement" programs for ordinary people—especially if they're Black—while ignoring the far greater government resources that flow to rich people through tax breaks and subsidies for businesses and homeowners.

Many liberals rightly reject this cruel view that the only functions of the state should be repression and corporate bootlicking, and instead assert that government can play a positive role in promoting human welfare. They hold up the decades after World War II as a model, when rich people and corporations paid much higher taxes, unions were at their peak, and a social safety net was created through programs for the poor, sick, unemployed, and elderly.

But let's think twice about proclaiming the postwar era as a

* Legal historian Gregory Ablavsky makes this argument in his article "The Savage Constitution."

golden age to be re-created. This was a period in which US policy was to create whites-only suburbs and Black urban ghettos, persecute hundreds of thousands of communists, bring the world to the edge of nuclear war, and destroy Korea, Vietnam, Guatemala, and Iran through wars and coups. Then there's the fact that the United States was enjoying the greatest economic boom in world history—which made it possible for rich people to be more generous without seeing their own wealth decline—only due to the unique circumstance that every other industrial country had just been bombed to smithereens. That's not something we should count on—or hope for—recurring.

The point is that even in the golden age of American liberalism, the government was not an agent of the people. It certainly is not now, when it imprisons a larger proportion of its people than any nation in the world and strategizes with oil companies about how to brutalize and lock up the heroes trying to save our planet by blocking pipelines. In recent years, the US government has used the Espionage Act against whistleblowers, like Edward Snowden and Chelsea Manning, who go public with information about domestic spying and war crimes, respectively. As defenders of these courageous resisters have noted, espionage is generally defined as passing secrets to the government's enemies. Since Snowden, Manning, and other whistleblowers weren't charged with leaking documents to Iran or China but to the general public, what does that say about how the US government regards its people?

Until the movement to defund and abolish immigration and police departments, few of the debates between Republicans and Democrats about the size of government took up the growing powers of the largest and most violent government agencies.* When Donald Trump boasted he could shoot someone in broad daylight without losing support, many were horrified that he would turn the country into a dictatorship. But that's precisely what hundreds of low-level

* It also must be said that many socialists should be louder in calling for defunding and abolishing the US military, which spends more than the next nine largest militaries combined while creating only turmoil and stalemates. It's basically the Manchester United of global imperialism.

police and border patrol officers do every single year, which should tell us something about the authoritarian society we live in right now. Some of us more than others.

Strangely, many of the people who are most into tracking elaborate conspiracies that supposedly take place inside the "deep state" have no problem with the violent crimes that are openly committed by the brutally shallow state known as your local police department. Nor do they often have a problem with obvious real-life US government conspiracies like voter suppression and overseas military coups. And while many of us are increasingly worried about the secret plots of Facebook, Google, and other tech companies to record our conversations and track our movements, conspiracists seem happy to spend all their waking hours being spied on by Silicon Valley trackers, as long as they can spread their bogus memes about pedophilia rings and vaccine hoaxes.

Conspiracy theories are supposed to offer forbidden alternative perspectives to freethinkers who refuse to accept mainstream disinformation. If fact, they are all variations of an ancient and simplistic story about good guys coming together to fight against the hidden forces of evil—only with convoluted and shape-shifting plotlines that string people along until their mistrust of authority has turned into blind faith in con artists and dictators. It's a temptation that exists across the political spectrum. In the early 2000s, some antiwar activists preferred to see the September 11 attacks as a Pentagon "false flag" operation rather than one of the many unpredictable but inevitable consequences of the United States waging war across the planet. More recently, it's been conservatives who have gravitated toward wild fantasies rather than deal with how climate change and COVID expose the problems of capitalism.

The spread of dangerous lies about election results and vaccines is alarming, but lecturing people to "believe science" and other appeals to have faith in authority aren't helpful. Popular conspiracy theories often connect with some aspect of people's experience with lying government agencies or pathologically greedy corporations. It's a healthy instinct to not trust the people in charge of a capitalist society. Where conspiracy theories go wrong is that they give the people at the top way too much credit for actually knowing what the hell they're doing. The reality is scarier: the US government, powerful and destructive as it is, is a servant of the thick ooze of capital, which has no master plan other than making more of itself.

The US Department of Defense, for example, is well aware that global warming is the biggest threat out there. It has funded extensive studies and military scenarios preparing for food riots and refugee rampages. But it doesn't occur to the most powerful military force in world history that there is something it can do to thwart the threat of climate change itself. Generals could be planning the invasion of the boardrooms of oil companies to order them to switch energy production to solar and wind. Instead, they are waging and planning wars to keep the oil flowing and the temperature rising. No matter how many brilliant scientists and strategists it employs, the Pentagon maintains the mindset of a street cop—concerned only about keeping order for the bosses.*

Just as capitalism combines the tyranny of the individual owner with the anarchy of all the bosses' competition with each other, it combines the repression of each ruling elite over its subjects with the chaos of their competition with every other ruling elite for control of global trade and military dominance. *Imperialism* is the term socialists use for this global anarchy among states, and it includes everything from warfare to diplomacy to trade agreements, whatever can give one nation a leg up in what the English used to call the Great Game.† For all of the growing central and secret powers accruing inside the government, we don't even get the benefit of that power being used for rational purposes.

Some of our most dangerous conspiracy theories are fueled both

---

* At the very least, the Pentagon could cut down on its own greenhouse emissions. There is no institution in the world that consumes more oil than the US military.

† Specifically, "the Great Game" referred to the nineteenth-century British rivalry with Russia for control of Central Asia. This smug name for a century of wars and horrors is a great illustration of the English penchants for understatement, dry wit, and genocide.

by those who spread them and those who deny them in words but whose actions seem to tell a different story. Most Democratic politicians, for example, loudly denounce those who claim climate change isn't real, while they also continue to approve oil and gas drilling in a way that makes you wonder if they actually believe their own words. This in turn leads more people to assume that the crisis can't actually be that bad, and that maybe Republicans are correct that Democrats are exaggerating or flat-out lying about climate change for some evil reason or another. Conspiracy theorists may think of themselves as deeply cynical, but their problem is that they still naively think that politicians are smart and in charge, whereas the more accurate and simpler explanation is that they are corrupt idiots who are selling out humanity's future for the sake of their careers.

Socialists aren't immune to the appeal of conspiracy theory—it's an occupational hazard for people who like to hang out in dark bars and talk ominously about "the ruling class." In the leadup to Donald Trump's election, more than a few of us found ourselves using the conspiratorial *they*—as in "*they* won't let this asshat win and bring down the richest country in the—would *they*?"

We shouldn't have been surprised. Capitalists are a strange ruling class. For most of written history, the same elite getting rich from the labor of slaves and peasants was also in charge of their health, education, and protection, with no artificial distinction between "economics" and "politics." But today the capitalists in control of society's most impactful decisions—whether to burn more oil, close another factory, starve the school system of tax funding—don't think they are responsible to anybody but themselves and their investors. Many of them didn't want the most powerful country in the world to be run by an erratic weirdo who would do anything the shouting people on Fox News tell him to. But those concerns mostly ended once it was clear that the stock market wouldn't crash. Now if Bernie Sanders had won the presidency, you can bet the capitalist class would have quickly discovered its sense of civic duty and mobilized its vast economic power against the diabolical threats of universal health care, environmental regulations, and workplace democracy.

It's been a while since Americans believed in the Capitalism-Democracy fairytale, but until Trump many took solace in the fact that while our political system may be corrupt and broken, at least that gave it a kind of stability that prevented despotism. Now we've seen that we can have the worst of all worlds. Capitalism puts so much power and wealth in a few hands that from our point of view down below those hands seem to wield complete control, but in fact the people in charge of shaping the world for our children often have no clear plan beyond the next election or quarterly earnings report. They veer from crisis to crisis, from disastrous invasions and global financial meltdown to denying countries vaccines during a global pandemic. No matter how badly they screw up, capitalists always seem to find solutions to their crises at our expense. They'll send more troops, close more hospitals, normalize previously unthinkable numbers of deaths, whatever it takes—unless our forces are strong enough to stop them.

Most of the time we aren't, and the cynics among us conclude that there never was a crisis. Some go even further and wonder if the whole thing was a conspiracy, dismissing those who dare to fight as powerless pawns being moved around a chessboard. They may find that fatalism comforting, but they're wrong. The crises are real, and they can prove to be capitalism's undoing—if there is a viable alternative waiting to replace it.

Damn, that would have been a great cliffhanger if the title of the book hadn't spoiled it.

PART III

SOCIALISM

PROFIT
SYSTEM

6.
WORKERS' POWER

In October 2013, workers at the Bay Area Rapid Transit (BART) system went on strike, complicating the daily commute for employees of San Francisco powerhouses like Google and Twitter. Tech company executives who like to think of themselves as rebellious "disruptors" of old economic models were furious that they had been disrupted by what they considered the most outdated relic of them all—a labor union.

"Get 'em back to work, pay them whatever they want, and then figure out how to automate their jobs so this doesn't happen again," fumed Richard White, the CEO of something called UserVoice, whose website boasts that it helps organizations "find a better way to listen to their users' voices."

Clearly, Richard White wasn't in the mood to listen to the voices of BART workers that morning, perhaps because they were reminding him that even Silicon Valley can't run without train operators and bus drivers. Like all capitalists but more so, tech bosses prefer to imagine that society has no classes, only millions of individuals freely buying and selling their goods and labor to one another. If a few of them have more money than they can spend while most of us have more needs than we can afford, the rest of us shouldn't get jealous. Just create the next big app and join them!

The BART strike punctured this fantasy by reminding our Captains of Digital Industry that the working class is real. Even worse (for them), the next decade would see major strikes hit the region's schools, hotels, and hospitals. And then in 2018, the strike bug breached the mighty digital fortress of Google itself, where employees staged a global walkout to protest sexual harassment. This unprecedented action took place in the midst of an equally historic national strike of Marriott hotel workers that won landmark protections against the threat of sexual assault from guests.

These job actions against sexism are part of a larger trend that has seen social justice movements enter into the workplace, where they have the potential to reach new levels of power: Teachers demand immigration protections for their students; entertainment company employees rally against anti-trans company policies; software developers demand their companies end contracts with the military. The overall state of labor organizations is still weak, but these actions show that working-class power isn't just a fading memory but a potential twenty-first-century powerhouse whose strength comes from unity, solidarity, and other old-fashioned ideas that bosses like Richard White thought had been replaced by algorithms and machines.

Always Classy

Until the recent socialist revival, class was an unmentionable topic in polite American conversation. Even now, when the word is uttered on television it is usually following "middle." Everyone in the United States is supposedly middle class, whether we make $30,000 a year or $300,000 a year. It would be unpatriotic to let ourselves be divided by that extra zero.

In the national mythology, one small segment of society is The Rich and a slightly larger one is The Poor.* By default, everybody else is in The Middle, which is useless for understanding class but great for disguising it. If everyone is middle class, then millions of daily episodes of class conflict—between managers and managed, landlords and landlorded, and so on—become just so many random personality beefs.

If we wanted a more accurate picture of the middle class and

---

* Most poor Americans are white, but you wouldn't know that since media discussions of poverty are usually illustrated with images of Black people. So even when we're supposedly discussing class, we're talking in code about race.

divided the US population into three income levels, the middle third would live in households that make between $45,000 and $100,000 a year. This at least gives us a better sense of reality than television, where *Two Broke Girls* can apparently afford a swanky Brooklyn apartment with hardwood floors that in the real Brooklyn would be home to "Two Bankers' Kids."

Income doesn't capture the full story of wealth, however. For the superrich, only a small portion of their wealth comes from their salary—most of it is based in what they own, from mansions and stock market investments to top-secret immortality elixirs extracted from the tear ducts of endangered tigers. For the rest of us, our financial status comes partly from our weekly paycheck but even more so from our levels of homeownership, which are shaped by what just might be the most racist institutions we have.* For nearly a hundred years, banks and real estate companies have tied home values to the racial demographics of the area, forcing African Americans to pay more for homes that sell for less, with devastating consequences. The salaries of African Americans are 60 percent of the salaries of white people, which is bad enough. But thanks to the racism of the real estate industry, the total wealth of Black households is only a catastrophic 10 percent of that of white households.

But measuring wealth alone doesn't give us a full understanding of class. Throughout history, classes have been defined more by what they do than by how much they make. The categories of peasant, merchant, landowner, slave, craftspeople tell us something about people's wealth and much more about the role they play in society. This is still the most useful way to understand class, although it's understandable why many rich people would rather we not.†

---

* "Most Racist American Institution" is a highly competitive category with no shortage of worthy contenders, including the criminal justice system, the medical establishment, and country music charts. But it's hard to deny the prize to banks and real estate agents. Read Ta-Nehisi Coates' "The Case for Reparations" on the history of Black people's exclusion from homeownership through the practice of "redlining" and Keeanga-Yamahtta Taylor's *Race for Profit* on how this injustice has continued into the present day.

† For instance, instead of "rich people" we could say "monopolists" or

Classes are categories based on the roles different groups of people play in the ongoing production and reproduction of their society's needs and wants. In the US and other wealthy nations, capitalist society has three main classes*:

- Capitalists, who own what Marx calls "the means of production," meaning the wealth that they use to invest in land and tools to create more wealth (that is, profits);
- Workers, whose labor the capitalists have to buy because land and tools can't turn themselves into profits;
- A middle class of managers, professionals, and small business owners, whose work combines aspects of both capitalists and workers.

These classes are not defined by income. When autoworkers unionized in the 1930s, many of them went from making poverty wages to owning second homes and motorboats over the course of a generation, but they were still autoworkers.† Today if a Starbucks worker goes on strike, she'll probably find less support from her district manager making $60,000 than she will from an airline pilot making twice that much. That's because the manager makes his money by helping Starbucks keep labor costs down while the pilot is a union member who can relate to fighting alongside one's coworkers against a company trying to squeeze them for more profits. Although

---

"parasites" or "inheritors of vast fortunes who squander wealth that should be taxed for the public good on doomed startup investments in testosterone-infused sports drinks."

* Across the world, poor farmers are a very important part of global capitalism, with complicated class dynamics between those who own their own small plots of land and those who are agricultural laborers forced to work for others.

† Sadly, these days new hires in the auto industry are making wages much closer to the miserable pre-union level of pay. But as autoworkers they still have the power to win back their old gains—if they can relearn some of the lessons of how socialists built the labor movement last century. Sorry, I forgot to mention that socialists built the labor movement—no biggie. Check out Sharon Smith's *Subterranean Fire* for the overall story or Farrell Dobbs's *Teamster Rebellion* for a participant's account of the incredible 1934 Minneapolis general strike.

it's true that, as we learned in kindergarten, we are all snowflakes with our own unique personalities, it's equally true—and not taught in school—that many of our opinions and basic political instincts are shaped by our class experiences. As a result, each class has its own distinct characteristics.

The point of dividing society into these classes is not to neatly assign everyone to their proper category, which is impossible. A handful of pro athletes make more money than many CEOs, but they also remain workers—as they are reminded when they dare to question a coach's decision and the press screams at them to "Shut up and play!" More commonly, nurses and teachers face speedups and harassment like other workers but still retain some of the middle-class status and decision-making power that their jobs used to have before health care and public education were corporatized. The most effective nurses' and teachers' unions are the ones whose members fully understand that they are no longer—if they ever were—professionals working in partnership with their hospitals and school boards but skilled workers being exploited by them. These examples show that class cannot be oversimplified, not that class isn't a useful category. In fact, they demonstrate one of the key characteristics of class: conflict with other classes. Each class can only be defined in terms of tension-filled relationships to the others.

The paradox of working-class power is that it originates in how individual workers are powerless. We sell our labor to a boss because we don't have a choice, not because we enjoy giving up our autonomy for eight to ten hours a day. As sociologist Erik Olin Wright explains, workers only exist as a class because they or their ancestors have been robbed of the land and wealth that would allow them to survive independently. But it is this individual powerlessness that eventually compels workers to come together and organize collectively.*

When people mention the working class, they often simply mean people who don't have much money. Socialists define workers not by

* *Eventually* is a convenient word for authors because it can mean strikes will break out next month or next decade. If you're waiting for the class struggle to explode, pack a lunch.

what they lack but by the potential power they possess. When workers sell their labor, they are put to work in large complex organizations—factories, hospitals, stores, distribution centers—which they operate collectively. This complex division of labor allows relatively small groups of workers to produce or make possible huge productivity and profits—or jeopardize them by going on strike. Those few thousand Bay Area transit workers can cause a much greater economic disruption than a similar number of poor farmers or Walmart managers.

Some complex organizations are harder places for workers to organize themselves. Most unions were born during an era when tens of thousands of workers were concentrated in factory districts in large cities. Today many factories have been moved to isolated rural areas, and companies like Uber and FedEx have created complicated structures designed to reclassify drivers as "independent contractors" instead of workers entitled to labor rights. But workers are working toward overcoming these obstacles. In recent years, employees who were thought to be impossible to get organized have been doing just that. Starbucks and Amazon workers have created their own unions. Fast food workers have held sit-ins and strikes to win raises. Restaurant *deliveristas*, many them undocumented immigrants, have mounted their delivery bikes to shut down traffic and won legal protections from wage theft and abusive conditions. These scattered victories may only affect the conditions of a relatively small number of workers, but you can bet they're kicking off hushed conversations among many more.

As individuals, members of the middle class enjoy more autonomy than workers, which is why many workers dream of escaping their class to become managers or open up their own businesses. But as a collective, the middle class is pushed around by capitalists just like workers, only without the collective power to resist. The paradox of working-class power applies to the middle class in reverse. The very individualism of the small business owner who "doesn't have to answer to anybody"—which is celebrated as a core American value and envied by many workers—makes the middle class extremely ineffective as a collective body. In times of widespread class struggle, the middle class is like a gang of big toughs squaring off against an army regiment: it's outmatched in terms of both discipline and firepower.

"What is the middle class in the middle of?" asks Michael Zweig in *The Working-Class Majority*. "If we answer this question in terms of power instead of income, we see that the middle class is in between the two great social forces in modern society, the working class and the capitalist class." The middle class occupies a murky region where elements of capitalism's two defining classes intermix. "The independent peasant or handicraftsman is cut up into two persons," writes Karl Marx in *Capital*. "As owner of the means of production he is a capitalist; as laborer he is his own wage-laborer."

Because the middle class contains traits of both workers and capitalists, it sees itself as the "everyman" representing all of society—as opposed to the "special interests" of workers (the actual majority of the country) and big capitalists. This is true in the sense that the middle class best represents within itself the class contradictions of capitalism, but that doesn't help it find a way out of those contradictions. Without the individual power of capitalists or the collective power of workers, the political instinct of the middle class is to simply call on both sides to stop yelling at each other. These appeals for unity serve as useful window dressing for maintaining the status quo, which is why the middle class is an excellent breeding ground for politicians.* Most elections feature two candidates competing over who can more sincerely pose as an ordinary middle-class guy, as if that is more important than which capitalists are funding their campaign and writing their platform.

But at certain dark moments in history (like . . . *ahem* . . . now) the paradoxical middle-class instincts for both unity and extreme individualism—and its frustration with its own weakness—make it a breeding ground for far-right ideas and even fascism. Because of the widespread confusion of class with education levels, cultural identification, and ethnicity, the media will often describe white militia

* Of course, there are also super-wealthy politicians like Donald Trump and George W. Bush who have somehow managed to present their own stupidity as a culture war against the intellectual elite.

members as "working class" even when they are office managers, franchise owners, and herbal supplement lifestyle influencers.

The working class, by contrast, has the power to back up its words with action, but it only gains this power through a long process of learning how to organize itself. A hotel cleaner is struggling to keep up with the crazy pace of forty room changes a day. She pleads her case to the manager, who tells her if she's not happy, she can find another job. A few months later, she comes back to his office, this time with the other fifteen cleaners on her shift. Suddenly the manager is more interested in his workers' unhappiness, particularly because he knows that with every minute they are standing in his office, the hotel is falling further behind the fast pace of room changes that he had been so proud of until this very instant.

The group nature of working-class resistance doesn't just help workers to extract some raises and better conditions from their bosses. It can also, in much more intense moments, point to a possible world without bosses, which makes workers different from many previous exploited classes. When peasants revolted against the big landowner and took over his estate, they usually divided it among themselves into individual plots of land—a fine plan for them that happened to not challenge the larger system of private land ownership. By contrast, if the hotel workers find themselves in a fight in which they have to take over the hotel—perhaps to prevent it from being closed—they wouldn't split the rooms up into a hundred separate new hotels but would instead have to all run the operation together, which would force them to come up with a new collective decision-making structure. Even if these workers are no more interested than peasants in challenging private ownership, the nature of their class pushes them in that direction.

There are hundreds of businesses in the United States—and around the world—that are owned and run by workers. These cooperatives aren't socialist—they exist inside a capitalist economy and have to compete for profit with other companies or get driven out of business. But they do provide proof of a basic reality that is clear to most workers every time their manager takes a sick day: things run a lot better when there aren't bosses around to bark orders that alternate between being dead wrong and dead obvious.

Most people think socialism is a set of laws that would more equally distribute wealth. That's part of it, but laws that reduce inequality don't eliminate bosses, who can elect or overthrow the governments that pass those laws, as we've seen many times over. The essence of socialism is that workers can use the collective organization that they have learned under capitalism to create not just cooperative workplaces but a cooperative society geared to meet humanity's needs instead of a competitive one geared to maximize profit.

Poor capitalists. In order to make profits, they must bring workers together and exploit them, but competition with other capitalists forces them to push that exploitation further until the workers resist and create their own organizations whose very existence demonstrates that workers are capable of running the place themselves and calls into question what right capitalists have to own it in the first place. It is this process of inadvertently uniting millions of members of the lower classes into an organized working class that led Marx and Engels to famously pronounce in *The Communist Manifesto* that for all its new technologies and products, what the capitalist class "produces, above all, are its own gravediggers."* At the time it was an epic burn, which was one of Marx's specialties.† A hundred and fifty years later, with capitalism very much alive, it can read more like an empty boast.

The working class hasn't managed to bury capitalism yet, but Marx wasn't wrong to say that it could—especially because there were many socialists in his time who actually opposed workers' struggles. These were the utopians who understood the socialist project as one of dreaming up a harmonious society so obviously superior to this nasty one that people of all classes would join together and make

* Years ago, I stood on a picket line of cemetery workers in Queens, New York, torturing myself with all the nerdy Marxist signs I could have made.

† If Marx were a 1980s action star, he would have been great at those post-kill one-liners:
Hey Karl, what happened to that factory owner?
He got hit with an Invisible Hand.

the dream a reality. The utopians were mostly middle-class reformers who sympathized with workers' plights under capitalism but viewed strikes as pointless protests that would only push away the factory owners who needed to be convinced to join the socialist cause.

Marx came from a middle-class background himself, yet he viewed class conflict not as a neutral observer but as a participant on the side of the workers. Like the utopians, he recognized that the class struggle produced by capitalism is a hard road with more defeats than victories. But he understood that the solution was not to wish the struggle out of existence but for the working class to win it and build a more just society. The great Black abolitionist Frederick Douglass made a similar point about the struggle against slavery:

> If there is no struggle there is no progress. Those who profess to favor freedom and yet deprecate agitation are men who want crops without plowing up the ground; they want rain without thunder and lightning. They want the ocean without the awful roar of its many waters. This struggle may be a moral one, or it may be a physical one, and it may be both moral and physical, but it must be a struggle. Power concedes nothing without a demand. It never did and it never will.*

The simplest definition of Marx's version of socialism is that it is what society would look like if the working class were in charge. Workers' cooperative organization would extend across industries and society. Equally important, the majority class would be in power for the first time in recorded history, which would lead to the gradual dissolution of classes themselves, since a majority can't live off the exploited labor of a minority (for the same reason that pyramids don't work upside down). This idea that socialism is defined by the ultimate victory of the working class is Marx's most important contribution, because it showed how socialism could develop from being a fantasy dreamed up in smoke-filled dorm rooms at 3:00 a.m. (or whatever

---

* An office manager I once worked for had a "*Without struggle, there is no progress*" brass plaque on his desk. It makes me wonder if there is some company that specializes in turning icons of the Black freedom struggle into employee motivational slogans: *File that paperwork—by any means necessary!*

the nineteenth-century version of that was) to an ambitious but sober program rooted in the agency of a real social force created by capitalism itself.*

Solidarity

Just to be clear, we are talking about potential, not describing reality. Some people think it's enough to discredit socialism by pointing out that most workers today don't agree with it, which is a bit like disagreeing with great sex on the basis that many people don't have it. But our claim isn't that a majority of workers are usually socialists, just that they can become committed to socialist ideas at certain historical moments (more on this in chapter 8).

"Workers of world unite! You have nothing to lose but your chains." It's one of Marx's greatest quotes, but not one of his most accurate. Injustice has always relied on the bitter irony that the less people have, the more afraid they are to lose it. The fact that billionaires own eight thousand times as much as us should make us revolutionary, but instead it often makes us conservative, focused on maintaining the little we've got—whether that's a decent job with benefits or the entitlements of being a white man or a US citizen.

How could we expect workers to set their sights as high as seeing their class running society, when they're told every day of their lives that they aren't worth a damn? From childhoods in underfunded schools to adulthoods in underpaid jobs, working-class people are taught to keep their heads down, follow orders, and keep their bright ideas to themselves. Then we turn on the TV to watch CEOs and action heroes celebrated for being free-spirited, rebellious, and every other quality that's been drummed out of us. This is one of capitalism's nasty habits: degrading people and then blaming them for their degradation. Black men are the last workers hired and the first ones

---

* Not that Marx was above some youthful debauchery. Two years after he wrote the *Manifesto* and was living as an exile in England, Marx and a few German friends went on a pub crawl that involved a near-bar fight, smashing streetlights with cobblestones, and getting chased by London police.

fired, and then are demonized as deadbeat dads who don't provide for their children. Girls are vilified for dressing the very way they've been told to by a thousand magazine covers; as adults they'll be blamed by those same magazines for neglecting their families to go to work, even while they are punished at work for taking time off for their families.

The working class isn't immune to this drumbeat of negativity. Like all human beings, we are great at thinking bad things about ourselves—and even better at thinking them about others. As we discussed in chapter 4, capitalism is a system that produces racism and sexism alongside smartphones and Happy Meals, and workers can buy it all just like everyone else. Walk outside an office tower on a summer day while bankers and delivery guys stand together objectifying the passing women, and you'll see that the bonds of class are not automatically stronger than those of gender. That's why it's a serious mistake to try to avoid supposedly "divisive" issues like abortion rights and transgender equality in the belief that this will prevent workers from uniting around economic demands.* Issues of freedom and dignity matter just as much to people as the size of their paycheck. If some workers ignore—or support—the oppressions of other workers, then real unity is impossible.

Many later socialists have criticized Marx for downplaying how much racism, nationalism, and other oppressions would prevent workers of the world from coming together. In fact, Marx wrote more about these issues than some people realize—particularly in his later years as he saw the effect of British imperialism in India and Ireland—but that's less important than the larger point that workers aren't automatically on the same team. Working-class unity is not something to be proclaimed by ignoring racism, xenophobia, and other oppressions within the working class but something to build by combatting them. Some critics claim that socialists prioritize class struggle over issues like racism and sexism, but most of us see them as inseparable—and

* There's a special circle in lefty hell reserved for activists who dismiss the importance of oppressions they don't experience. Perhaps an eternal planning meeting where cis men are repeatedly flicked in the balls as a demon yells at them to stop being distracted and "focus on the real issues."

we have a proud history of fighting oppression. In the 1930s, for example, thousands of members of the Communist Party USA did pathbreaking and courageous work against segregation in the South. It was so effective that for decades afterward antiracism and communism were viewed synonymously by southern bigots, who called civil rights activists "communists"—and communists racist things that I won't put into print.*

Marx saw the working class as a "universal class" that could represent the interests of all people. If the largest and most exploited class takes power, he argued, it will have no choice but to create a society without class and exploitation. But there is more than one path toward universality. In the 1970s, Black feminists formed the Combahee River Collective, named after the site of a daring Civil War raid by Black soldiers that freed over seven hundred people from slavery and burned down a number of slave plantations.† Combahee members argued that socialist unity could only happen if it included the leadership and demands of Black women, whose struggles against economic, racial, and gender injustice gave unique insights into the workings of capitalism. Using logic similar to Marx's, their founding statement argued, "If Black women were free, it would mean that everyone else would have to be free since our freedom would necessitate the destruction of all the systems of oppression."

They weren't the first Black women to note the ways in which racism and sexism combined to create new forms of oppression—an idea that Kimberlé Crenshaw would later name *intersectionality*. But the women of Combahee and other Black feminists like Audre Lorde

---

* A couple of great books about some of the Communists' antiracist work in the 1930s are *Hammer and Hoe* by Robin D. G. Kelley and *Communists in Harlem* by Mark Naison. For a first-person account, check out Hosea Hudson's autobiography, *A Black Worker in the Deep South*.

† The raid was commanded by Harriet Tubman. Just so we're clear, a formerly enslaved woman with no military training can pop in to the military for a few months and bring actual freedom and justice, but put that same army under the command of five-star generals and all it will deliver for decades is drone bombs on Afghan weddings and fat checks for weapons manufacturers.

and bell hooks showed how their societal position could make Black women—as well as other female, trans, and nonbinary people of color—vital agents of revolutionary change.

The phrase that Combahee coined, "identity politics," has sometimes been taken to mean that only those suffering from an oppression should be part of the fight against it. Many radical women of color formed separate organizations because, as Combahee cofounder Barbara Smith later put it, "We were marginalized in Black contexts [and] white feminist contexts. We needed to have a place where we could define our political priorities and act upon them."* But their strategy for political change was to build coalitions and argue for a genuine unity that put the demands of the most oppressed first.

There are many debates among socialists about the usefulness of identity politics. As Olúfẹ́mi O. Táíwò points out in *Elite Capture,* many movements have seen more privileged members of an oppressed group assume leadership positions and then use their identity as a shield against necessary and criticism. But Táíwò argues that this is an inherent problem of capitalist inequality that infects identity-based movements in the same way it does everything else. Identity politics doesn't have magical powers to prevent co-optation and distortion any more than socialism does. But in the 2010s, the vision of the Combahee River Collective started to bear fruit. Young activists of all genders and races have been profoundly shaped by the analysis of socialist Black women like Angela Davis and Keeanga-Yamahtta Taylor, and many of our most dynamic protest movements and campaigns have been led by women, trans, and nonbinary people of color.

From the anti-slavery movement through today, the Black freedom struggle has usually been the leading edge of resistance in the US, not because African Americans are a majority but because their oppression is so central to the structure of US capitalism. The same can be said about Indigenous struggles in Canada and Latin America—and increasingly in the US (as we'll discuss in the next chapter). In recent years, many countries have also seen women and queer people play a

* Smith's quote is in an interview in *How We Get Free,* Keeanga-Yamahtta Taylor's oral history of the Combahee River Collective.

leading role in galvanizing opposition to right-wing governments. Protests against sexual assault and abortion bans, from the massive "women's strikes" in Chile, Argentina, and Poland to the less durable but still important Women's March and #MeToo movement that greeted Trump's election in the US, have shown the key role of feminism in any movement for freedom.

Socialists aim to win workers to fighting against oppression on the basis not of sympathy but of solidarity: the idea that this fight is in our mutual working-class interests. Solidarity is a deeply moral concept, but not in the way we usually think about morality. Because capitalism is based on ruthless individual competition, most people think that being a good person is about self-sacrifice, and that our motives aren't pure if we're benefitting in any way. Not surprisingly, this can cast doubt on the sincerity of any good deed—as any online comments section will demonstrate. But when people get together in spaces that aren't controlled by social media companies trying to manipulate our emotions, it's easier to find all the ways we stand to benefit from working together—even though that means confronting serious issues of inequality inside our movements.

One of the best expressions of solidarity came from the great railroad union organizer and socialist leader Eugene Debs, when he stood before a court that had convicted him of speaking out against the First World War: "Your Honor, years ago I recognized my kinship with all living beings, and I made up my mind that I was not one bit better than the meanest on earth. I said then, and I say now, that while there is a lower class, I am in it, and while there is a criminal element, I am of it, and while there is a soul in prison, I am not free."

Beautiful words, but they are only remembered because they were backed up by a lifetime of actions.* Solidarity is an idea, but it is also something that takes time to build, a network of relationships based on the trust that if I stand up, you will have my back. *Pride* is a great

* Eugene Debs was a beautiful man and the most important socialist in US history. For a short intro, look up Howard Zinn's "Eugene Debs and the Idea of Socialism." If you like irreverent and sometimes foul-mouthed comedy, listen to *The Dollop*'s two-part podcast on him.

movie about the slow process of solidarity-building between London LGBTQ activists and coal miners during their epic 1984–85 strike. It begins with a small handful of queer activists—many of whom had radical politics and working-class backgrounds—trying to find a miners' union local that would accept donations from a group that called itself "Lesbians and Gays Support the Miners," which wasn't easy back in the mid-1980s. But they showed their sincerity by raising serious money for the strike in the gay community and driving out to Wales for regular picket line visits. A year later, the miners made the return drive to London to march alongside their new comrades in the Gay Pride Parade (this is way before Pride was mainstream), which gives the movie a nice Hollywood ending that happens to be completely true.*

Working-class solidarity against oppression is possible because all workers experience oppression, although they may not always feel it in their daily lives. As Rosa Luxemburg once put it, "Those who do not move do not notice their chains." At home on the couch, workers are just as likely as anyone else to buy whatever crappy ideas this society is selling. When they find themselves in a struggle, they make connections between themselves and others facing injustice. Some white workers, for example, may begin to think about how the way management harasses them for no reason is similar to what their Black coworkers face not only from the boss but also the police.

One of the struggles that inspired me to become a socialist was a multiracial three-year strike in the mid-1990s, at the Staley corn sweetener factory in a conservative area in southern Illinois. As the strike went on, many workers grew frustrated with their union's lack of a strategy and started going out on their own to build community support. When Black workers organized a contingent in the local Martin Luther King Jr. Day parade, dozens of their white coworkers joined them, the first time almost any of them had participated in an MLK Day event. Within a few months, they were organizing a march to commemorate King's assassination, chanting "Black and white, united we fight!" These white workers might have initially reached

* Except for the miners' strike going down to crushing defeat and the leading activist dying of AIDS. Spoiler alert: the eighties sucked.

out to Black organizations simply to build support for their strike, but they came away from the experience understanding that the fights for labor rights and civil rights are connected.

"It's not the struggle for flat-screen TVs that motivates white unionized workers and a fight for dignity and justice that drives low-wage Black and immigrant workers," writes union activist Amy Muldoon. "There is a longing for justice throughout the working majority in society that goes unnamed as long as our identity as working-class people and the oppression we suffer as a consequence is hidden."

Take This Job and Shove It

At a time when the number of strikes and the size of unions is still at historically low levels, people looking to fight oppression and injustice may find the idea that the workers will lead the way to be outdated and naïve. Many of those doubters are themselves workers. The strength of a class can have less to do with its numbers or even wealth than its awareness of itself (something socialists call "class consciousness"). As workers come together to fight in their own interest, Marx once wrote, they change from being a class "in itself" to one that is consciously "for itself." Conversely, when working-class unions and parties are weak, actual workers disappear from public view, often replaced by the blue-collar caricatures of "real Americans" so beloved by political and media elites.

There's a lot of public discussion about how the "white working class" is becoming more conservative while "coastal elites" are becoming more liberal, but it's much more complicated. In the last decade there's been a partial revival of strikes and workplace protest, primarily in jobs like teaching and nursing, as well as those among university workers, media, and most recently tech. The result is an increase in class consciousness and feelings of solidarity among people with college educations who don't match images of "the working class" as being made up of blue-collar white men without college educations. Those people are also part of the working class, of course, but there have been few successful strikes and a steady erosion of labor rights in the factories and warehouses where many of them work. As a result, there has been an increase in some of these workers turning to the politics of scapegoating and nationalism. What appears to some as a polarization between classes is more a reflection of a cultural and political gap being widened by very different levels of class struggle happening inside the working class.

It's true that the working class has undergone major changes. Within the United States, some factory work has shifted from more unionized northern cities to rural areas in the South and West, and others have been moved overseas. Many jobs have been replaced by machines, just as the San Francisco CEO gleefully hoped. But let's not exaggerate these trends. The global working class is bigger than it has ever been. What is often called deindustrialization is really a process in which industry hasn't disappeared but changed, with more factory jobs involving knowledge of computerized machinery, and production centers relocating to places without unions in the United States and around the world.

Pundits regularly dismiss unions as insignificant relics of the past, until a strike erupts and they freak out about how much chaos it will cause. Even then, they are often incapable of actually listening to the workers they now realize they depend on. "Get 'em back to work, pay them whatever they want, and then figure out how to automate their jobs so this doesn't happen again." Richard White assumed the BART transit workers were striking for more money, but in that strike the key issue was maintaining work rules and worker control over job assignments—the same autonomy that any CEO would expect as a given.

Most labor disputes are as much about dignity as they are about pay. This rarely comes across in news coverage that is bent on portraying striking workers as greedy for putting their own interests ahead of customers who may be inconvenienced by a strike. In fact, the Taft-Hartley law made it illegal for most workers to strike over issues that affect customers, other workers, or the general public, which is a major reason why the US hasn't seen the powerful general strikes that have happened in many other countries.* Yet for some reason, the

---

* After Taft-Hartley was passed in 1947 by a Republican Congress, President Harry Truman and the Democrats campaigned on a promise to overturn the law. A strong voter turnout by union members led

press and politicians who scold unions for only looking out for themselves never call for changing labor laws to allow them to go on strike for others. When Chicago teachers struck in 2012, some of their main concerns were the city's huge class sizes and deteriorating school buildings. The mayor told them that those weren't legal bargaining issues—and then denounced them for not caring about the children.

A few months after the BART strike, transit workers at the Long Island Rail Road in New York threatened to walk out, sending political and business leaders into a tizzy. What really baffled them was that the workers were not upset about their own pay and benefits but about proposed cuts for future hires. This principle of fighting for future workers is widely understood by union members, who sometimes call it "protecting the unborn"—which we can only hope even further infuriates those in management who are also anti-abortion. The experience of struggle and solidarity gives the working class a very un-capitalist understanding that our struggles are linked to past and future generations. But this is a strange and infuriating concept for bankers, bosses, and business owners who have never experienced collective labor. The idea of workers sacrificing today's wages for the sake of preserving a standard of living for people they don't even know tomorrow strikes them as crazy. That's why these are exactly the people who shouldn't be in charge of making long-term decisions about our planet.

In the early seventies the US media frequently covered a trend they dubbed "blue-collar blues": young workers influenced by the protest movements of the sixties who were tired of the bleak world of factory life. The mood was captured by the #1 country music hit "Take This Job and Shove It," and epitomized by a 1972 strike by autoworkers in Lordstown, Ohio, where the main issue wasn't money or benefits but assembly-line speedups. The local union leader said that his

---

to Truman winning reelection and Democrats getting both houses of Congress. But then, wouldn't you know it, enough Democrats broke ranks to prevent Taft-Hartley from being repealed. Truman acted all mad, but he went on to use the law twelve times to break strikes. And for decades every Democratic presidential candidate has promised unions that he would repeal Taft-Hartley . . . and it's still here. THIS . . . IS . . . WHAT . . . THEY . . . ALWAYS . . . DO.

members were striking for the right to be "able to smoke, bullshit a bit, open a book, daydream even." It was a glorious echo of the 1912 Lawrence textile strike's famous "Bread and Roses" demand for both higher pay and dignity on the job—although, sadly, Lordstown hasn't gone down in history as the "Bullshit and Daydreams" Strike.

Then a global recession hit, the 1980s unleashed a wave of union busting that never stopped, and everyone stopped talking about the blue-collar blues, even as the speedups only got more intense in the coming decades. Instead, we were all supposed to be grateful to the generous "job creators" who give us paychecks, and then work overtime and get second jobs to make up for those checks falling further and further behind the rising cost of living. For forty years, income inequality went up, unionization rates went down, and it seemed the downward spiral would never end . . . hang on a second.

It might have just happened.

It's far too early to tell, of course, but I'm writing this book during a wave of pandemic-driven union organizing at Amazon warehouses and Starbucks stores, as well as strikes against mandatory overtime at factories that have been able to impose conditions that would have made workers' heads explode at Lordstown in 1972.* Perhaps even more historic is the Great Resignation of 2021, in which one in four workers quit their jobs before the end of the year. This widespread rejection of crap jobs (readers of the footnote below will nod at that choice of words) was brought on by the COVID crisis, which pushed millions to quit rather than risk their health in unsafe workplaces, and millions more who were stuck at home, to reassess their priorities. The resulting labor shortage has pushed workers' wages up by almost 6 percent—with far greater increases for those working in restaurants, transportation, and warehouses.

Large numbers of people quitting their jobs for individual reasons is very different from large numbers of people taking collective action

---

* Amazon delivery workers are squeezed so relentlessly that bathroom breaks are often not an option. Some of them have reported shitting into bags as they speed in their vans on the way to bring customers their packages—perhaps with a bonus delivery of Hepatitis C.

to go on strike. Still, for the first time in half a century, millions of US workers have taken actions that prioritize the health of loved ones over the demands of managers—and then seen real material improvements based on their ability to withhold their labor. This is bound to have a generational impact.

Ideally, there would be massive protests happening all the time. But the working class inherently finds itself at a disadvantage. In his great little book *Why Marx Was Right*, Terry Eagleton finds an analogy to our current situation in an old Irish joke about someone who is asked the way to the railroad station and responds, "Well, I wouldn't start from here." Socialists, Eagleton says, might feel the same way about today's low level of class struggle. "But there is, of course, nowhere else to start from. A different future has to be the future of this particular present."*

The working class at this particular present has low levels of unionization but rising levels of solidarity and rebellion. That wouldn't be a bad starting point if we had the luxury of more time. Instead, the climate crisis requires new thinking, some of which is actually very old.

---

* Eagleton's book is a great follow-up for readers who like this book but would prefer one that is wittier, smarter, and better written.

7.

LAND BACK

One of the most common questions about socialism is what we might call the toothbrush question: *There's no private property at all? People have to share literally everything?!?*

Given that the average American is currently over $90,000 in debt, most of us might want to consider what is actually *our* property, as opposed to something a bank is letting us have until we get laid off or have an accident and they show up to take it away. But the toothbrush question also assumes that shared property is such a bizarre concept that people won't know the difference between factories and hospitals that should be commonly owned and little things like your underwear that, believe me, nobody wants to share. Let's give humanity a little more credit.

The word *socialism* was first used in the early 1800s, but societal models based on equality and communal living are far older. Just about everywhere around the world has had traditions of land and other vital resources being collectively owned by the community. It has been one of capitalism's primary missions to wipe this practice off the face of the earth. One of the earliest of these efforts was the fencing off of common grazing lands in England. That produced a rebellion led by people who came to be called The Diggers, who sound like a 1970s soul group but were in fact some of the forerunners of modern communism. The Diggers organized occupations of formerly common land in the belief that land was "a common treasury for all" as their leader Gerrard Winstanley put it. There was no mention of anyone having to share their toothbrush, although if there's any truth to the old cliches about English people's teeth, that might not have been an issue.

In 1969 Garrett Hardin wrote an influential essay called "The Tragedy of the Commons," which claimed that the English common lands were doomed to fail because individual users ruined the commons through overgrazing. For Hardin, an anti-immigrant crusader who supported population control measures against the poor, the lesson was that too many people ruin everything. For free market fans who misunderstood Hardin's essay, the point was that anything other than private land ownership leads to chaos. For all of them, the actual history of common lands was irrelevant. In fact, as Nobel Prize–winning economist Elinor Ostrom and others have proven, many commons, from 1600s England to today, have been successfully and sustainably managed.

In the twenty-first century the commons are having a major comeback in activist circles. Affordable housing advocates are pushing for community land trusts, which allow people to own their own houses but on land that is held in common by all members of the trust in order to keep prices affordable. Digital activists fight to preserve the "internet commons" from telecommunications monopolies and government censors. Scientists are pushing to establish commons for everything from seeds to DNA in order to prevent corporations from being able to patent and privately own foodstuffs and our own genetic material. And many socialists organizing around climate change argue for an "energy commons" so that renewable energy like wind and solar wouldn't be owned by corporations but would be shared by all, just like the air and sunlight that produce them.*

As a framework that is literally rooted in common sense, the commons is a great way to think about the socialist approach to sustainability and collective ownership—and why nobody is interested in taking your toothbrush. But even the best ideas are powerless without the societal force to overcome the opposition of ruling-class interests that stand to lose from them. Remember Marx's argument that it was

---

* Ashley Dawson's *People Power: Reclaiming the Energy Commons* is a great resource for understanding the idea and organizing efforts.

the working class, and not utopian blueprints for a more rational society, that could win an alternative to industrial capitalism. Today, the fight to create new commons requires the strength and leadership of those who have best been able to preserve the old one: the world's nearly four hundred million Indigenous people.

Just as the working class contains the potential to lead society toward democratic control of our labor and the wealth it creates, Indigenous peoples have the potential to lead society toward a sustainable relationship to nature and its gifts. Actually, forget "potential." Indigenous communities are actively leading the fight to save humanity and other life from climate change and other environmental disasters. Globally, Indigenous people make up 5 percent of the population but live on lands that contain 80 percent of the planet's estimated species. This is not a coincidence: Indigenous people don't just happen to live in the same parts of the world that have the most species of plants and animals. They have energetically protected ecosystems from capitalist and colonialist invasion and destruction because they understand their connection to their natural surroundings in a way many others don't. A 2021 study found that Indigenous resistance to fossil fuel projects in the US and Canada over the past decade had prevented greenhouse gas pollution that was the equivalent of almost a quarter all the total annual emissions from those two countries.*

One of the most hopeful elements of these scary times is that this is a historic moment of Indigenous resurgence, radicalization, and leadership. Around the world, from Southern Africa to Ecuador to North Dakota, Indigenous peoples have been leading the fight to defend Earth through pipeline blockades, courtroom battles, and everything in between. Through these campaigns, which build on their historic and ongoing resistance to being annihilated or assimilated by global capitalism, Indigenous peoples have been building

---

* The study is called "Indigenous Resistance Against Carbon." In more grim news, a report that same year by Global Witness found that Indigenous people made up over a third of those killed for protecting the environment. These murders almost all took place in the Global South but pipeline protesters in North America have also faced brutal repression.

a set of ideas and organizations that point the way not back to some imaginary past but to the only livable future.

The key to this fight is and always has been land. We can't rebuild a commons for the twenty-first century on stolen ground. Restoring Indigenous peoples' sovereignty over and stewardship of their territories would both correct a five-hundred-year wrong that haunts us all and put more of the Earth under the protection of those most qualified for the job. "Organizing around Native land rights," argues Indigenous environmentalist Dina Gilio-Whitaker, "holds the key to successfully transitioning from a fossil-fuel energy infrastructure to one based on sustainable energy."*

#LandBack is a demand and hashtag that burst into popular awareness in the 2020 wave of Indigenous-led blockades and occupations in Canada, galvanizing First Nations peoples and their supporters across North America. Like "Black Lives Matter," "Land Back" is both a cleverly broad slogan and a framework for numerous local demands—from Lakota national sovereignty over the Black Hills (and the closure of Mount Rushmore) to Ojibwe rights to hunt and protect wolves in Wisconsin.

What does "Land Back" really mean? One answer comes from a *Reservation Dogs* episode that opens with a white couple driving past a sign that's been tagged with "Land Back" graffiti. "What do you suppose that means?" asks the husband. "They want the whole damn thing back? That's just not possible. I could see some of it back. You reckon that's what they mean? Some of it back? Or all the damn thing?" As he's arguing, he gets so distracted that he crashes into a deer, and the show returns to its regular Indigenous characters. The driver is asking the question that all non-Indigenous Americans have when they first encounter the demand: Do you

* This is from Gilio-Whitaker's *As Long as Grass Grows: The Indigenous Fight for Environmental Justice, From Colonization to Standing Rock*. In addition to Gilio-Whitaker and the other writers I mention in this chapter, I recommend Nick Estes's *Our History Is the Future: Standing Rock Versus the Dakota Access Pipeline, and the Long Tradition of Indigenous Resistance*, as well as Rebecca Nagle's *This Land* podcast and the *Red Nation Podcast*.

mean some land back or all of it? To which *Reservation Dogs* simply offers a deadpan, "Yes."

"Land Back" is a call to recognize that every inch of countries like the United States and Canada rightfully belongs to Indigenous people. A very first starting point is learning about and acknowledging the peoples whose land you are currently on and the ways it was taken from them. I live, for instance, in the ancestral homeland of the Lenape, who were expelled by Dutch and then English settlers and now live in communities in Oklahoma, Kansas, Wisconsin, New Jersey, and Canada. Land Back is also a practical struggle over relatively small but significant allotments that is winning tangible victories. The Esselen Tribe of California that had been exiled from its land for 250 years recently worked with environmental groups to purchase a twelve-hundred-acre ranch to build a traditional village and nature preserve. That same year the Yurok Tribe of Oregon finally won the removal of four dams on the Klamath River to restore the river for the salmon and those who live off them. Just as I was writing this chapter, the Wampanoag tribe—the people whose brutal suppression by the Pilgrims has been gaslit by the bogus story of Thanksgiving—finally won a fifty-year struggle for a small land trust in Cape Cod that will provide much-needed economic development.*

One of the key tasks for socialists today is to support Land Back in all its manifestations, and figure out ways to build a powerful global alliance of the working class and Indigenous peoples and a politics of respect and gratitude for the twin miracles of land and labor.

Living with the Land

There are various attempts to limit or expand what it means to be Indigenous for one cynical reason or another. At one end is the long history of US government refusals to recognize individuals and entire

* For the real history of the Wampanoag, listen to the *Red Nation Podcast* interview with Mashpee Wampanoag Vice Chairwoman Jessie Little Doe Baird.

nations as Indigenous. At the other is the absurd claim of some Israelis that their occupation of Palestinian land isn't really an occupation because according to the Bible all Jews are indigenous to the region.

Most Indigenous peoples don't define themselves by DNA testing or even by having lived somewhere for a long time. Instead, Indigeneity is often understood through a people's distinct "place-based" history and culture. Here's how Gilio-Whitaker puts it:

> The very thing that distinguishes Indigenous people from settler societies is their unbroken connection to ancestral homelands. Their cultures and identities are linked to their original places in ways that define them: they are reflected in language, place names, and cosmology (origin stories). In Indigenous worldviews, there is no separation between people and land, people and other life forms, people and their ancient ancestors whose bones are infused in the land and whose spirits permeate place.

The brutalities of conquest and capitalism have painfully wrenched many Native peoples away from these ancestral homelands to distant reservations or cities. Native American reservations today cover just 2 percent of the Indigenous land that makes up the United States. And yet through centuries of dogged resistance, many Indigenous people have maintained physical and cultural connections to their original lands and built relationships with their new ones. In a famous 1977 speech to a Canadian government committee looking to build an oil pipeline through his people's territory, Dene leader Phillip Blake gave a generous and inspiring vision of what Indigenous leadership has to offer the world:

> If our Indian nation is being destroyed so that poor people of the world might get a chance to share this world's riches, then as Indian people, I am sure that we would seriously consider giving up our resources. But do you really expect us to give up our life and our lands so that those few people who are the richest and most powerful in the world today can maintain their own position of privilege? That is not our way. . . .
>
> We have lived with the land, not tried to conquer or control it or rob it of its riches. We have not tried to get more and more

> riches and power, we have not tried to conquer new frontiers, or outdo our parents or make sure that every year we are richer than the year before.
>
> We have been satisfied to see our wealth as ourselves and the land we live with. It is our greatest wish to be able to pass on this land to succeeding generations in the same condition that our fathers have given it to us. We did not try to improve the land and we did not try to destroy it. That is not our way.
>
> I believe your nation might wish to see us, not as a relic of the past, but as a way of life, a system of values by which you may survive in the future. This we are willing to share.*

Blake meant that the Dene hadn't tried to "improve" the land in the capitalist sense of increasing its short-term yield or property value, but that instead they and other Indigenous peoples have sought to give back to the plants, animals, and landscapes on which they depend, and to make important decisions based on the long-term interests of what Haudenosaunee (or Iroquois) refer to as the next seven generations. As the Potawatomi botanist Robin Wall Kimmerer puts it in *Braiding Sweetgrass: Indigenous Wisdom, Scientific Knowledge, and the Teachings of Plants*: "In the settler mind, land was property, real estate, capital, or natural resources. But to our people, it was everything: identity, the connection to our ancestors, the home of our nonhuman kinfolk, our pharmacy, our library, the source of all that sustained us."

Indigenous people may not have sought to "improve" land for the sake of boosting its value, but there is a long history—documented in the opening chapter of Roxanne Dunbar Ortiz's wonderful *An Indigenous People's History of the United States*—of their significantly altering natural environments with agriculture, road building, and irrigation in ways designed not to conquer the surrounding world but

* This quote is in Glen Couthard's *Red Skin White Masks: Rejecting the Colonial Politics of Recognition*, a history and analysis of the struggles for sovereignty for Canada's First Nations, Inuit, and Metís. These movements, particularly the Idle No More movement that started in 2012, have had a major impact on the Indigenous radicalization inside the US that led to the Standing Rock fight.

enrich it. These historical examples, along with current ones such as the Menominee Nation's world-renowned model of sustainable logging on their land in Wisconsin, demonstrate Blake's point that the rest of the world treats Indigenous peoples as "relics of history" at our own peril. Indigenous people don't live outside of capitalism and its mandates to exploit and destroy the natural world. But in withstanding the genocidal assault on their culture, community, and knowledge, Native peoples have developed the most coherent ideas about living sustainably within our natural limits.

Okay, it's time to call out the elephant in the room. The main argument of this chapter—that Indigenous people have a central role to play in all of our survival and liberation—is also an acknowledgment that the much larger numbers of non-Indigenous peoples haven't proven ourselves capable of mobilizing to stop the slow-motion civilizational car crash that is global burning.

In the last chapter, I argued that the working class has the potential to strike down this system at its profit-making heart, and organize to create a more democratic and humane alternative . . . someday. The existential question, of course, is whether that day comes before capitalism has made the planet inhospitable for any type of thriving human society. Millions of workers and many unions have taken part in climate protests around the world, including the historic 2019 "Climate Strike" that brought millions of people out into the streets across the world. But we already know that protests alone aren't enough to change the capitalists' deadly calculations to continue burning fossil fuels. That will take the kind of massive economic disruptions that can only come from actual strikes, the kind led by workers that shut down factories, warehouses, and pipelines. This type of action is very difficult—and in the US possibly illegal, thanks to our old friend Taft-Hartley. But history has been made many times by working people's willingness to break the law, and besides, Taft-Hartley can't explain why there also haven't been major strikes against climate change in other countries.*

---

* Which isn't to say there aren't labor activists trying to change that. Look up Trade Unions for Energy Democracy to find out more.

A condescending explanation for the lack of class climate struggle is that most workers don't understand climate change or are too selfishly concerned with their narrow daily lives to focus on long-term planetary issues. A more accurate one is that many people depend on climate-heating jobs for a living, or are too overworked and overwhelmed by living paycheck to paycheck to get involved in a fight over more distant or abstract issues. I'd much rather hang out with the person giving the second answer, but both take for granted something that is in fact odd: why are most of us experiencing the slow suffocation of the planet that gives us life as something distant and abstract, a news item that we can choose to acknowledge or ignore?

If one of my kids were ailing the way many species of animals and plants are ailing, I wouldn't be able to ignore, deny, or put off the issue—no matter how stressed or busy I was. If they were running a fever of almost two degrees the way our planet is—if their vital systems were showing signs of contamination and failure over a period of months and years—I wouldn't need to be told by a doctor that something was wrong because I would already know through my close observation of and love for my child (well, the younger one at least).*

But I don't have that relationship with my planet, or the animals, plants, and rivers that give me and my kids life. I may imagine that I can "feel" something is wrong during a flood or heat wave, but I only know about climate change because of what scientists report (and yes, that's better than not feeling a relationship to nature and also *not believing* what scientists report). Nor do I have any intuitive sense of what it means that among the millions of forms of life on this planet, species are dying off at a rate thousands of times higher than they were a few hundred years ago. I know that's bad, obviously, and if one of them is an animal I've heard of, I'll feel shaken—but mainly because it makes me frightened about what that means for my own species.

Simply put, I am alienated from the non-human world. I understand that I depend on nature but don't intuitively feel a connection to it. There is something intellectually stunted about me and many others, a damage that has been a long time in the making that can't

* Just checking if you're reading, LJ!

help but impact our understanding of the damage being done to the world and ability to save it. "Over the last five centuries," explains Daniel Wildcat:

> Some of humankind brought tremendous change to life on the planet, and the change seems essentially guided by an allegedly objective mechanical worldview that envisioned the noblest human activity is the control of nature (the machine) and the forces of nature. We now find that the complex life of Mother Earth demonstrates that such a view is naive and dangerous, for we are situated, in spite of however much we would like to think otherwise, inside, as but one part of the life system of planet Earth.

I realize that many of you might be less alienated from nature than a guy in a Queens apartment where any wildlife sighting besides my cat is going to be a cockroach that will send me running for a paper towel . . . okay my shoe . . . okay a baseball bat. But living in rural areas or spending every weekend hunting or mountain climbing doesn't undo the effects of a culture that can only understand nature as a bunch of things to be exploited or experienced. Most of us see land as something to live *on* rather than, as Phillip Blake put it, something to live *with*. But not all of us.

The Comeback

In 1900, the total Indigenous population inside the borders of the United States had fallen to less than 250,000 people. Today there are almost four million American Indians, Alaska Natives, and Native Hawaiians—and many more who claim partial Native ancestry. "The history of American Indians in the twentieth century," says Gilio-Whitaker, "is the story of a comeback from the brink of almost total annihilation."

It's a comeback not only in terms of population but cultural and political influence. A major turning point in the global recognition of the need for Indigenous leadership came at the 2010 World People's Conference on Climate Change and the Rights of Mother Earth in Cochabamba, Bolivia. A decade earlier, Cochabamba had been the site of the historic "water war" protest movement that halted a plan to hand over the city's water supply to the American corporation Bechtel and inspired movements around the world against the turning over of water rights to private corporations. The water war was also an early example of the coalitions of socialists, unions, and Indigenous forces that would later win national elections in Bolivia and across South America, in what became known as the continent's "Pink Tide" of left-wing governments.

At the 2010 conference, thirty thousand people came together for a historic gathering hosted by Bolivia's first Indigenous president, Evo Morales, an Aymara protest leader whose party had come to power after years of protest movements led by Bolivia's Indigenous majority. A year earlier at the Copenhagen climate talks, the leaders of wealthy nations scoffed at the claims of Morales and Venezuelan president Hugo Chávez that capitalism was to blame for climate change—and then proved their point by failing to come to any new agreements. Environmental activists demoralized by this pathetic failure were therefore doubly inspired by the People's Agreement of Cochabamba that was ratified by the 2010 conference.

In what history may judge as the Pink Tide's most important legacy, the agreement set far more aggressive goals for reducing carbon emissions than anything government leaders had agreed to, but more importantly it created a framework for strengthening the social forces necessary to achieve those goals. People's Agreement of Cochabamba called for migration rights for those fleeing climate disasters, increased Indigenous representation at global climate negotiations, and climate reparations from the rich countries responsible for global burning to help poorer countries restore their forests and develop renewable energy infrastructure. The People's Conference didn't have the power to enforce these demands, but it has shaped the aspirations of climate activists around the world, and pushed many environmental organizations to understand the need to ally with Indigenous and anticolonial movements.

In 2016, Native people inside the US had their own Cochabamba moment, at the Standing Rock protest encampment to prevent the completion of the Dakota Access Pipeline. The pipeline was slated to pass under the Missouri River, endangering the drinking water for millions and creating a dire threat to the ecosystem, sacred burial grounds, and sovereignty of the reservation of the Hunkpapa Lakota, or Standing Rock Sioux Tribe. The months-long occupation at Standing Rock brought together thousands of Native Americans from hundreds of nations across the country. It also drew in many non-Natives as well, including four thousand veterans who arrived to defend the encampment—many of whom took part in a ceremony with tribal elders to apologize for the US military's crimes against their peoples.

The Standing Rock occupation won a temporary victory when the Army Corps of Engineers denied approval for the pipeline to cross under the Missouri River, but that was soon overturned by the new administration of Donald Trump. But the rallying cry of Standing Rock, *Mni Wiconi* (Lakota for "Water Is Life") was a milestone for building Indigenous solidarity across the many hundreds of nations inside the US, and for popularizing the need in the wider environmental movement for both direct action and Indigenous leadership.*

Around the world Indigenous leadership is taking place not only on protests but in courtrooms and constitutional assemblies, where scholars and activists are fighting to establish legal rights for nature based on the South American Indigenous concept of *buen vivir*, or living well. *Buen vivir* is not about individual wealth or spiritual contentment—apologies to my readers who are life coaches and New Age gurus—but rather about people, other living things, and the Earth living well together.

And so just as the US Declaration of Independence declared that all men (ahem) have the right to "life, liberty, and the pursuit of happiness," Ecuador's people in 2008 approved a new Constitution that gives rivers, mountains, and forests the *right* to "exist, flourish, and

* There are 574 federally recognized tribes in the US, as well as many others that the federal government refuses to recognize—because the US has never stopped trying to make Indigenous people disappear one way or another.

evolve."* Three years later, Bolivia passed a constitution that enshrines the right of nature to not be polluted and "continue vital cycles and processes free from human alteration." This legal movement has spread to a number of cities and tribal governments in the US, from the "Lake Erie Bill of Rights" passed by voters in Toledo, Ohio, to the White Earth Band of Ojibwe's formal recognition of rights to the wild rice that is central to their history and identity. While these constitutions have presented new legal challenges to oil and mining projects, they haven't stopped the relentless push for more drilling and pipelines—another reminder that ideas are only as strong as the social forces that can back them up—but they are important paradigm shifts that can be built on around the world.†

Within the borders of the US, the important fights for Native control of land involve the enforcement of the over 370 treaties that the US government signed in its first hundred years with Native nations. The fact that the US has repeatedly violated these treaties and taken land legally granted to Native peoples doesn't reduce their importance—especially in an era when Indigenous nations are in a stronger position to fight for their rights.

In fact, the government has made (and continues to make) numerous attempts to terminate these treaties, only to be blocked by Indigenous organizing, because they provide an important legal foundation for fights over land, access to sacred sites and hunting ground, and many mining and fossil fuel projects. A central aspect in the Standing Rock struggle, for example, was that the proposed pipeline ran through land that is not part of the current reservation but is part of the 1851 and 1868 Fort Laramie Treaties between the US government and the Oceti Sakowin (or Great Sioux Nation). Millions of non-Indigenous Americans who supported the Standing Rock occupation were taught a lesson in why treaty rights are critical for everyone trying to stop global burning.

---

* The Declaration of Independence also complains about "merciless Indian savages," who presumably did not make it into the category of "all men."

† Perhaps even in the US, if someone can convince the Supreme Court that Roscoe Conkling once told a buddy that trees should have voting rights.

An Indigenous–Working Class Alliance?

That connection is critical because despite their impressive resurgence, Indigenous peoples don't have the numbers or power in most places to overthrow colonialism and capitalism on their own and begin a new era of sustainable civilization. That's why the future depends on an Indigenous–working class alliance. And here's where things get tricky, especially in societies built on stolen land.

Whether we are rich or poor, recent immigrants, or descended from those who sailed on the *Mayflower*, most of us in the US are part of a settler society, renting or owning property that was bought from someone who bought it from someone who bought it from someone who stole it. We can protest about the innocence of our ancestors, especially those brought here through enslavement, invasions, and famine, but this isn't a trial. As Vine Deloria Jr. put in *Custer Died for Your Sins*: "The white man must learn to stop viewing history as a plot against himself."*

Most of the world in the nineteenth and twentieth centuries experienced the massive theft of territory, resources, and dignity that was colonialism. In some places, like India under British rule or Japanese-occupied Korea, the local populations were reduced to second-class status (often with a lower third class added in to better divide and conquer) so that their land and labor could be more ruthlessly exploited. But in other places, such as Australia, Palestine, South Africa, Canada, and the United States, people have been subjected to what's known as settler colonialism: an ongoing process that aims to eliminate native peoples and cultures and replace them with colonizing "pioneers."

In North America, settler colonialism targeted Indigenous people both in order to get access to their land and to erase their communal way of life as a living example of alternative ways of living with nature

* For people of color, of course, US history has often been a nefarious plot. What Land Back means for African Americans in particular, who have suffered not only enslavement and segregation but repeated displacement from cherished lands and neighborhoods, is an important discussion for Black and Indigenous activists.

and one another. "Tribal land was tribally owned—tribes and private property did not mix," writes the historian Patrick Wolfe. "Indians were the original communist menace."

It's true that this settler society is divided by class, and that Natives and working-class settlers share a common enemy in the wealthy elite. But one of the depressing themes of US history is that these tensions have often only fueled more land theft and racist white populism. Roxanne Dunbar-Ortiz explains in *Indigenous People's History* how settler colonialism was the product of conflicts both between settlers and Natives and between rich and poor settlers: poor white farmers who were excluded from good lands dominated by wealthy slaveowners pushed west to take Indian lands, only to then be forced out by rich land speculators and forced further west, where the cycle would begin again.

There are clearly grounds for common cause between many Natives and non-Native workers, but to build that alliance we have to be honest about the real conflicts of interest. Settler colonialism isn't just a matter of what some socialists call "false consciousness," an awkward phrase that's meant to explain why many workers often fail to recognize what is in their best class interest. An example of this might be a worker with citizenship status who resents an immigrant worker for supposedly driving down wages, not realizing that the immigrant is only paid less because she is denied equal rights and that legalizing her status would benefit them both.* In contrast, non-Indigenous workers in settler countries aren't necessarily wrong to perceive a potential threat to their way of life from Land Back demands that might jeopardize jobs and homes that exist on stolen treaty lands.

Most socialists have always been aware of how land could divide the working class. Unlike the workplace, where workers are denied the individual solution of owning their own piece of the business (remember the hotel room example from the previous chapter), when it comes to land, there most certainly is an individual solution

---

* That was an extremely quick summary of a very important question. For much more, check out Aviva Chomsky's *They Take Our Jobs! and 20 Other Myths about Immigration*.

of private ownership, one that most workers understandably spend their lives working toward. Workers can't remain workers while also becoming the boss, but they can remain workers while being settlers, property owners, and diehard nationalists.

Marx and Engels, who spent most of their lives as exiles in England, bitterly complained about how the class struggle of English workers was weakened by their support for their bosses' colonialism in Ireland and India. The Russian socialist Vladimir Lenin went further and argued that the fight of workers against exploitation was not enough to win socialism. Instead he argued that the class struggle had to be combined with the resistance to colonial land theft, and that socialists in imperial countries like Russia would have to bring what he considered to be full socialist consciousness to their fellow workers by convincing them about the dangers of Russian (or English, German, or French) nationalism and the need to support oppressed minorities and nationalities like Jews and Ukrainians.

Many socialists have debated whether Lenin's argument about socialists bringing consciousness to workers was elitist.* But history has proved his point about the importance of anticolonialism, which has been at least as strong a factor as workplace conflict in the many upheavals and revolutions of the past century. And it might not be a coincidence that the most successful socialist revolution was the one in Russia, where Lenin's Bolshevik Party sought to be a "tribune of the oppressed" that united workers, peasants, and colonized people resisting the Russian empire. (Some might say being the most successful socialist revolution is like being the most artistic *Transformers* movie, but let's save that discussion for the next chapter.)

The thing about anticolonialism, though, is that, as the name

---

* This is from Lenin's famous *What Is to Be Done?* The book, a fierce argument about the kind of underground socialist organization necessary under an oppressive Russian monarchy, has been taken out of context by many anticommunists and treated as gospel by too many communists. It's a difficult book written for Russian socialists in 1901 and literally nobody else. And yet there are passages that are brilliant and strangely timeless, and I recommend reading it at some point, preferably in a study group with someone who knows some of the context.

makes clear, it's a force of resistance to a system that doesn't contain answers to what will replace that system. In the mid-twentieth century, new countries in Africa and Asia that won heroic independence battles against European colonial powers still found themselves trapped by a global capitalist economy dominated by a handful of wealthy nations that demanded cheap access to their labor and natural resources. Whether their leaders viewed themselves as socialist or capitalist, most post-colonial societies have struggled to free themselves from the familiar patterns of colonial inequality.

In the early 2000s, there was hope that the progressive Pink Tide governments in Brazil, Venezuela, Bolivia, and elsewhere might break out of this trap. For nearly a decade these administrations directed wealth produced from oil, mining, and agriculture exports toward programs for the poor that reduced inequality and won reelections in the face of tremendous hostility from local and international elites. But by making national development policy even more dependent on the exploitation of nature (a choice imposed on them by their countries' place in the global capitalist order), these plans further degraded the rainforests and rivers, alienated Indigenous peoples, and then left the economies ruined when global prices for oil and other commodities dropped in the global recession of the early 2010s. By the end of the decade, Pink Tide governments had lost of much of their mass support and were ousted (with varying levels of legality) by right-wing backlash.* The exception was Venezuela, where Hugo Chávez's successor Nicolás Maduro remained in power through a horrific economic collapse by relying on increasingly anti-democratic measures.

In countries like Ecuador and Bolivia, the experience of Pink Tide governments has led many Indigenous and environmental activists to conclude that mining and fossil fuels under any government are a form of "extractivism" that looks to colonize the land and people living on it. Anti-extractivism is an Indigenous-led politics that can hopefully provide future anticolonial struggles a stronger and more coherent set

* I'm writing this during what appears to be the start of a new left-wing wave in Latin America, but it's too early to know what its impact will be.

of aims.* But these efforts can only succeed if they win more support, which brings us back to the question of the working class.

The demand for Land Back today is critical for socialism, just as the anticolonial movement was during Lenin's time. It's not a perfect comparison, by any means. Movements for Indigenous sovereignty aren't nearly as destabilizing to capitalism as movements for national liberation were a hundred years ago. But the climate crisis is, and to meet that crisis we need both greater Indigenous control of land and increased awareness among working-class leaders about the destructive impact of settler colonialism.

Despite the obvious conflicts of interests between settlers and the Indigenous peoples whose lands they live on, there are also powerful potential bonds of solidarity—even beyond the interest we all should share in halting global burning.

In recent years there have been many coalitions built between Native and non-Native communities, sometimes overcoming longtime bitter local histories, to prevent energy companies from further destroying local ecosystems. One sign of the changing times is the experience of the Lummi Nation, which in the 1970s faced vigilante violence for claiming their treaty rights over salmon fishing in Washington State but more recently has united with settler fishermen to stop construction of a deep-water coal port. Perhaps the most well-known of these new coalitions is the cheekily named "Cowboy Indian Alliance" between ranchers and Natives in Nebraska, which helped block the completion of the Keystone XL pipeline. This alliance was built on the pathbreaking work by Lakota members of the American Indian Movement, who overcame bitter tensions with white ranchers to form the Black Hills Alliance that won major victories against plans for uranium mining in 1980. Marvin Kammerer, whose family had been ranching in the Black Hills since they were first taken from the Lakota explained to the *New York Times* how his sense of history had changed:

* Thea Riofrancos was a participant in many of these protests and then wrote the excellent *Resource Radicals: From Petro-Nationalism to Post-Extractivism.*

> I've read the Fort Laramie Treaty, and it seems pretty simple to me; their claim is justified. There's no way the Indians are going to get all of that land back, but the state land and the Federal land should be returned to them. Out of respect for those people, and for their belief that the hills are sacred ground, I don't want to be a part of this destruction.*

Short-term coalitions against specific projects are of course not the same thing as a long-term alliance against capitalism, and both the coalitions I just mentioned were opposed by workers in the fossil fuel and construction industries. This is why it's so important to win a strong version of the Green New Deal, which calls for a switch from fossil fuels to renewable energy that is put in place by well-paid and unionized workers. The GND, as it's known to its buddies, is an excellent starting point for getting us out of the "jobs versus the environment" debate that is completely nonsensical—converting power plants, factories, and transportation networks to renewable energy takes a lot of work, which when people get paid for it is known as jobs.

But the GND is just a general framework, which is great for starting conversations and opening minds, but also leaves it vulnerable to being watered down to irrelevance. Just as importantly, we should be clear that it's a national proposal for a global problem and, perhaps most importantly, doesn't take up the need to slow down production and consumption and fundamentally change our understanding of and relationship with the world around us. That's why Indigenous groups like the Red Nation have put forward proposals like "the Red Deal," which takes the Green New Deal as a starting point for pushing for the more comprehensive program initiated by the People's Agreement of Cochabamba.

Perhaps the best starting point for Indigenous–working class solidarity is removing the en dash I just wrote and looking to the Indigenous working class. For the sake of analysis, I've been treating class and Indigeneity as separate categories, but as with all discussions of categories like race, gender, and class, we should remember that life is

---

* Zoltan Grossman tells this story in *Unlikely Alliances: Treaty Conflicts and Environmental Cooperation between Native American and Rural White Communities.*

experienced intersectionally.

The working-class movement has always been energized, educated, and radicalized by the experiences of workers who face multiple forms of oppression that give them sharp insights about how different issues are connected. During the Black Power explosion of the 1960s and '70s, African American workers were at the heart of a US labor movement strike wave that targeted both speedups on the factory floor and discrimination in the union hall. The Women's March and #MeToo protests during the Trump years coincided with a historic strike wave of women-led teachers' unions, which won widespread public support with their combination of badass militancy and community-building. Hopefully, #LandBack and *buen vivir* will find their way into new currents in the US labor movement as they already have elsewhere in the Americas, raising new demands for sustainability and Native sovereignty and reviving some of the best labor traditions of fighting for future generations and resisting the bosses' relentless push for growth at all costs.

Recognizing that Indigenous people have a critical role to play against capitalism doesn't mean idealizing (and dehumanizing) anybody as morally or spiritually superior beings—any more than socialists should ever imagine that workers wake up every morning singing union songs and planning their next general strike. There were Native peoples who enslaved African Americans in the 1800s and Native nations that own oil companies today. Indigenous peoples are just as diverse and divided as anyone else, and they are saddled with even more historic impoverishment and trauma.

We are all influenced by a settler society that erases real Native people and uses their names and images to promote SUVs, health food products, and college football teams. Raised in this culture, even well-meaning non-Natives can confuse supporting and learning from Indigenous traditions with shopping for their own spiritual salvation in cultures they don't truly understand. So let's be clear that the goal of building solidarity with Indigenous peoples isn't discovering the meaning of life or paying less for therapy and anti-depressants. We'll just have to settle for saving the world.

There is a poetic beauty in the idea of a united force of Indigenous peoples and the working class: the gravedigger created by capitalism side by side with the gravedigger capitalism never managed to kill.* The strength of the working class is that the system needs it to create profit; its weakness is that it's always being created anew, torn from its history and natural surroundings, and susceptible to cooptation and division. The strength of Indigenous communities is their incredible efforts to maintain and build non-capitalist worldviews and organizational structures; their weakness is that they face the constant threat of elimination—whether that takes the form of genocide, laws that break up tribal lands, boarding schools designed to "take the Indian out of the child," or pipelines that destroy local ecosystems and access to sacred sites.

It's going to take more than poetry to bring these two powerful forces together. It will take Green New Deals and Cochabamba accords, plus many more water wars and Standing Rock defenses. These and other fights have demonstrated the importance of Indigenous movements to millions of non-Indigenous people—including many socialists.

The socialist movement has a mixed record at best on Indigenous politics. Far too many socialists, especially those in settler colonial societies, have accepted some version of the dominant ideology that views Natives as people from the past who are not an important part of the present and future. The wave of Indigenous-led struggles across the Americas has forced that to finally change.

It's one of many examples of how all of our ideas can change through our experience of struggle, which is good since a lot of ideas need to change very quickly. How can large numbers of workers be convinced of the need to support Indigenous demands and support a revolutionary fight against this system? Through a revolution.

That might seem like it gets the chronology wrong. We're taught to view revolutions as the final step of a plan carried out by radical

---

* Okay maybe not so much poetry as a classic movie featuring an unlikely duo that come together to get the job done, like Omar and Brother Mouzone in *The Wire* or Nicholas Angel and Danny Butterman in *Hot Fuzz*.

leaders, when in fact they are the process by which millions of ordinary people become radical leaders. But then so much that we learn about revolutions is backwards. It would probably take a whole chapter of a book to explore. Fortunately...

BEST SAFETYMATCH

8.

REFORMS AND REVOLUTIONS

In the clickbait era when there is no shame in lying to get our attention, the word *revolution*—like *unbelievable*! and *genius*!—is so overused that it loses all meaning. We're bombarded by ads that boast about *revolutionary!* advancements in stain removal and websites that *revolutionize!* how we buy our socks.

Occasionally across our screens we catch snippets of actual revolutions: swarming masses of long oppressed people suddenly finding the collective courage to face off in the streets against government forces—often armed with weaponry purchased from rich countries where citizens are encouraged to talk to their doctors about joining the revolution against erectile dysfunction. Foreign correspondents report on these conflicts in jaded tones that imply that all this is quite a spectacle but doomed to end badly. A real revolution, it would seem, is not cutting edge at all, but a throwback from an age that most of the world has thankfully outgrown.

And then, seemingly out of nowhere, it's June 2020 and the police murders of George Floyd and Breonna Taylor have tripped wires that are suddenly visible across the country. Twenty million people are marching in big cities and small towns in the largest protest movement in US history. Store windows are smashed and boarded up, liberal mayors are chased away from protests, cops and vigilantes stalk demonstrations with foaming rage. And everywhere people are suddenly discussing a question that would never before have even occurred to them: what would happen if we abolished the police?

All pretense of "law enforcement" melts away as police rampage against peaceful marchers in city after city, revealing the ugliness of raw state power to millions who had always seen cops as agents of public safety. A precinct is burned down to the ground in Minneapolis—and a poll shows that more than half the country thinks it's justified. Athletes refuse to play that day's game. Events are cancelled, one after another. Black rage, tightly suppressed for decades inside bodies wracked by headaches and hypertension, finally and once again come bursting out into a society under the illusion that it had moved past this type of thing. Life can't possibly go on as normal anymore.

Until it does. People can't stay out protesting in the streets forever. Politicians make promises. New polls show that most people find abolishing the police to be too radical. Things do return to normal, slowly at first and then ruthlessly, clubbing down the stragglers who didn't get the message that it's time to leave the streets. Within a few months, many can forget that anything ever happened. But others have been permanently changed, in numbers we won't know until the next eruption.

For historians, the word *revolution* can refer to many types of profound changes, including those like the "Industrial Revolution," that take place over decades or even centuries. In politics, it refers to a more condensed process in which large numbers of people go beyond the accepted norms of political action in order to change the government—sometimes creating an entirely new political or even economic system, more often just replacing who is in charge.

What happened in the summer of 2020 wasn't a revolution. But it was a reminder that the slow and patient work done over years by handfuls of activists can sometimes lead—in moments that are impossible to predict—to a sudden and unplanned societal convulsion, in which millions find themselves on the streets together and feel the incredible power they possess when they act in unity. A new generation was given a taste of what the Russian socialist Leon Trotsky meant when he said that a revolution is the "forcible entrance of the masses into the realm of rulership over their own destiny."

Revolutions, like relationships, usually end badly. To reject in advance the potential of revolution out of fear of the possible outcomes is the political equivalent of living a lonely and risk-free life in order to avoid rejection and heartbreak. That may sound hopelessly romantic, but so are socialists (romantic, that is, although often hopeless as well). We love people and think revolutions are the only time that most of us get to show how extraordinary we are—to the world and to ourselves.

It's been half a century since the 1960s revolutionary wave that swept the world from the slums of Algiers to the factories of Paris and Detroit.* Entire generations since then grew up cynical about political romance. The fabulous sixties slogan "Be realistic, demand the impossible" was replaced by self-help mantras about sticking to what you can control and not making demands of anybody but yourself.

That started to change in 2011, when revolutions exploded across North Africa and the Middle East. Millions who had suffocated for decades under monarchies and military dictatorships took over city plazas and refused to be moved. Across the globe, this "Arab Spring" rekindled romantic passions that had long been dormant. People everywhere were moved by the sudden transformation of what had been the world's most rigidly unchanging region.

But the regimes struck back. The uprisings were drowned in military repression in Egypt and Bahrain and civil war in Syria, Yemen, and Libya. The upheaval created space for counterrevolutionary forces like ISIS in the Middle East—and a racist reaction to Muslims and migrants in Europe and the US. Only in Tunisia did the revolution result in a more democratic government, and even there with questionable progress on social justice and economic equality. A decade later, many in the Middle East and beyond question whether there were any revolutions at all—or just some protests over-hyped by the global media.

---

* Three quick recommendations: Gillo Pontecorvo's "I can't believe this isn't a documentary" *The Battle of Algiers* about the Algerian revolution to win independence from France; Daniel Singer's *Prelude to Revolution* about the French general strike of 1968; Dan Georgakis and Marvin Surkin's *Detroit, I Do Mind Dying* about the League of Revolutionary Black Workers, the most important organization of African American revolutionaries you've never heard of.

This is the doubt that every counterrevolution in history aims to produce. Revolutions are not a single event but a long process of protests and repression, reforms and backlash, uprisings and many brutal defeats—each of which leads many to conclude that the revolution was a disastrous mistake that only led to more violence and chaos. These arguments win the day, until people remember that their normal lives are filled with violence and chaos AND hopelessness—and the revolutionary spark is lit once more.

What Makes a Revolutionary?

Growing up I never would have thought that I would become a revolutionary—and even now that's certainly not the first word I would use to describe myself.* Revolutionaries are supposed to march in the jungle in camo fatigues, while I'm chilling on a couch wearing my comfy pajama pants.† I don't have the confrontational personality you might associate with someone looking to upend the political system. But I am a revolutionary, not because of the way I dress, talk, or behave but because I believe there needs to be a revolution, and I do my best to act on those beliefs.

Before becoming a socialist, I thought revolutionaries preferred to talk smack rather than get their hands dirty in daily struggles like raising the minimum wage. I didn't actually know any radicals, but I was pretty confident in my assessment based on an extensive exposure to goofy sitcom characters and Hollywood movies about the 1960s. There are of course some very online types who sneer at important movements whose rhetoric isn't sufficiently revolutionary, and others who think that at every protest they are required to express their

---

* It wouldn't even crack the top three words that begin with the letter R: *resplendent*, *rakish*, and *ridiculous*.

† That joke is from the first edition of the book, before COVID and the global pajamas and sweatpants *revolution!* There might even be some tough-as-nails guerrilla fighter sitting around in her pajama pants, reading this book and getting pissed. Please don't come after me, comrade. I'm just a ridiculous, rakish, resplendent author trying to get some laughs.

contempt for capitalism by breaking a store window—even if it might hurt the movement in that given moment. But for most of us, being revolutionary is not a set of words, a style of protest, or what clique you sit with in the cafeteria. It's about understanding that capitalism inevitably produces revolutions, and doing what you can to prepare for them so that they might win.

The tricky part is that you don't know if that scenario might arise in five years or fifty. Revolutions don't just happen whenever revolutionaries want them to—the very nature of a revolution is that it's an uprising of far larger numbers of people than the minority who are always down to start something. I don't recommend standing outside the White House tomorrow with a megaphone demanding that the government surrender. Preparing for revolution in "normal," nonrevolutionary times doesn't mean stocking up on canned food and gas masks (in most places that's now called "summer shopping"). It means building political parties, worker organizations, mutual aid networks, and renewable energy cooperatives; creating study groups and free universities to recover the revolutionary history we are denied in school; and fighting to win better laws and union contracts that can both make the path to socialism a little easier and teach our side how to organize and win.

Many of these efforts fall into the category of reforms, the word socialists often use for important changes under capitalism that fall short of tearing down the entire political and social order. Some people have a misconception that revolutionaries reject organizing for reforms, either because we don't think they go far enough or, even more absurdly, because we're afraid that if people's lives improve, they won't want to get rid of capitalism. In fact, most of us spend our lives fighting for reforms. From reducing police funding in the local budget to passing Medicare for All in Congress, socialists prioritize incremental changes that will both make our lives immediately better (which, for the record, we are for) and strengthen the working class for the fights to come.

All this is pretty obvious, but confusion can arise because the socialist movement, starting with Rosa Luxemburg's famous pamphlet *Reform or Revolution*, has long identified a problematic trend known as "reformism." Reformism isn't the project of trying to win reforms (again, that's literally what we do all day) but a political strategy that rejects revolutionary change in favor of gradually turning capitalism into socialism through a process of piecemeal changes—generally through laws passed by socialists elected into office.

It would be great if this were a viable path to socialism, but capitalist democracy, which doesn't even let us decide whether a local hospital should close, isn't going to allow us to vote on whether to abolish the profit system. Here's how US secretary of state Henry Kissinger put it when the people of Chile voted in a socialist government: "I don't see why we need to stand by and watch a country go communist because of the irresponsibility of its own people." These weren't idle words: the US government supported a coup led by the Chilean military that on September 11, 1973, overthrew the democratic government and murdered tens of thousands of its supporters.*

Elections are a vital part of the path to socialism. The campaigns and congressional speeches of Bernie Sanders, Alexandria Ocasio-Cortez, and others have spread socialist ideas to millions in the US—and the path to socialism in many countries will likely involve both electing socialists and organizing to prevent those elections from being overturned. But that's just it: no ruling class in history has ever let itself be replaced without a fight, which is why successful socialist reforms and elections often only increase the need for protests, strikes, and even street battles. That's certainly been the experience in Latin America—not only in 1973 Chile but more recently in Bolivia, Ecuador, Venezuela, and Brazil—and US socialists better not look down their noses to their southern counterparts and think the same thing wouldn't happen here.

Even if it were possible for socialist leaders across the world to be elected and then disband armies, end poverty, and declare that Mardi Gras will now be held every Tuesday, the creation of socialist societies might still require revolutions. Think about how isolated and mistrustful most people are under capitalism. Many of us can't

* This is the 9/11 that we are meant to "Never Remember."

imagine our neighbors or coworkers getting together to organize a picnic, much less a society. It's only through the experiences of working alongside others to fight, for reforms and beyond, that millions of workers go through the learning process necessary to run society.

Marx once put it this way: "We say to the workers you will have to go through years of civil wars not only in order to change conditions but in order to change yourselves." By "civil wars," he was not necessarily referring to military battles but intense conflicts between classes that could take many forms—from workplace occupations to creating new constitutions to, yes, street battles with police or soldiers. These conflicts can involve not just pain and loss but the exhilaration of discovering previously unknown capacities and skills—as individuals, as a class, and as a society. Still, there's no getting around the fact that years of struggle is more of a bummer than peaceful elections and weekly Mardi Gras.

Most people who go to a protest, knock on doors for a radical candidate, or find themselves on strike are not at first opposed to the entire profit system. Yet once they step outside the path of their daily commute and engage in resistance—no matter how small—they often begin to see life from a different angle. Perhaps the local news distorted important details about the demonstration you were just on; how can you not wonder what other stories they are lying to us about? Or you spent months campaigning for Bernie Sanders only to see the leaders of his party unite to keep him from winning; now you're asking yourself if the Democrats are part of the solution or the problem.

Joining a protest can awaken other feelings that had been deadened over the years. You're out on strike when some coworkers leer at a woman walking past the picket line. Their everyday sexism didn't used to get to you that much because it was part of the general garbage of work that you ignored. Now that you're in a serious fight for your health care, however, you're not in the mood for it. You start thinking about the other sexism you've put up with because it doesn't bother you "too much." You explain all this to your coworkers in a few choice words, and some of them listen more closely than they normally would, because they know they need everyone to stick together to win the strike.

Even the briefest experience of resisting exploitation or oppression can be a life-altering moment, like finally discovering what it feels like to breathe clean air after a lifetime of pollution. A few years ago, 250 UPS workers in Queens walked off the job in response to an unjust firing. After a long fight, the fired driver got his job back, but the 250 each lost ten days' pay. Most of them took it as a victory, which speaks volumes about the meaning of solidarity. I got to know one of the workers pretty well. "Those 250 guys didn't just walk out for the fired driver," he said. "They walked out for themselves. For those ninety minutes we were out there in the parking lot, we felt freedom." He told the story at a socialist meeting, a place he might never have imagined himself before having his worldview rocked by abruptly finding himself in an intense class conflict.

In revolutionary situations, that change in perspective of one worker happens to millions as they experience what power feels like for the first time and begin to process what that means about the entire lives they have been living and what it could mean for the lives they will lead afterward. In the magnificent *Prelude to Revolution,* Daniel Singer describes the profound psychological impact of the events in Paris in May 1968, when students took over the streets and workers went on the largest strike the world had ever seen.

> When the productive machine grinds to a halt, the cogs themselves begin wondering about their function. When there is no gasoline, when public transport has come to a halt, when there is no smoke coming out of the factory's chimney, no normal work in the office, when the usual rhythm of social life has broken down, can the human mind alone stick to the routine? Do you remember those rare sleepless nights when, lying uncomfortably awake, you vividly recollect the hopes or illusions of youth and set this promise against the fulfillment, when with painful lucidity you ponder the meaning of your life? Something of that kind all at once happens to thousands, and it happens during the day. Only this collective blues is coupled with collective hope, is really inspired by it. The prospect of change releases the inner censorship. It prompts one to confess that the present is intolerable, to admit it to oneself but also to others. In factories, in offices, groups gather to discuss what can be done.

This is the beginning of a revolutionary situation, a joyous and disorienting mass feeling that's happened many times and in many places. The danger is that while the regular people are out in the streets having conversations for the first time since they were kids about what the world should look like, the people who are usually in charge of those matters are plotting how to bring things back to normal as soon as possible. These are the moments when the actions of large socialist organizations can have historic consequences.* In 1968 France, the Communist Party steered the strike wave out of the streets and into government negotiations, where all momentum was lost. In Tunisia 2011, leaders of the left-wing union federation were preparing to play a similar role, but were ousted by members who threw the union's crucial support behind the overthrow of the dictatorship.

There is so much to learn from every one of these moments, which is why many socialists nerd out over history. Our intense debates replaying little known details of past uprisings are sometimes mocked as cosplay, as if reading multiple books about the German Revolution of 1918 is little different from pretend-jousting at a Renaissance Fair. There are legitimate reasons to laugh at socialists, believe me, but this isn't one of them. Revolutions may be rare, but they're not random. Each one has so much to teach us because they reveal deep truths about capitalist society that normally are hidden.

Scientists study tectonic earthquakes not only to predict when future earthquakes can occur but also because they are rare opportunities to study the interaction of plates that normally can't be observed because they are grinding away deep under the surface of the planet. So it is with revolutions and social classes. Workers are usually so busy being exploited and oppressed that they appear to have little interest in the major political questions of the day, much less the ability to solve them. But the seismic shift of revolution reveals that the class has more depth than was visible from the surface. Suddenly workers are intensely debating every aspect of how society is run and using their

* Note to my fellow socialists: these moments are very rare, and you are probably not currently experiencing one, so stop torturing yourself about how to respond to that tweet.

new committees and councils to act decisively on those debates. At the same time, the bosses who just yesterday were unquestioned leaders now stand naked in their powerlessness before the world, because their workers are no longer following their orders. All the while, middle-class leaders who used to confidently think they represented all of society careen desperately back and forth between whichever of the two contending classes seems to offer a way out of a conflict in which they can only see chaos.

Just as our placid physical surroundings have been shaped by glaciers crashing through mountains and lava bursting out of flat earth, our seemingly stable landscape of laws and borders is the result of tremendous upheavals, whose successes and failures have shaped the peaks and valleys of our political aspirations. Slavery is unacceptable because the Haitian Revolution made it so. Democracy is preferable to monarchy thanks to the legacy of revolutions in England in the 1600s and France in the 1700s. The ability of rich countries to directly dominate poor ones has been weakened by revolutions in Mexico, Cuba, and China and strengthened by counterrevolutionary coups in Chile, Congo, and Indonesia.*

Revolutions are a recurring and critical component of history, but they are usually taught in school as avoidable tragedies, with an emphasis on what went wrong to let this happen. This is why the most exciting period in US history—the period after the Civil War known as Reconstruction—is somehow the most boring chapter in most of the textbooks. Rather than telling the story of how former slaves battled the KKK and took political control of parts of the South before being sold out by their northern white allies, students yawn through a decade of arguments between Congress and the White House where nothing much seems to happen.†

---

* Since I just casually reeled off revolutions and coups in nine different countries, I probably ought to make at least a few recommendations for further information. For the good news, there's Adolpho Gilly's classic *The Mexican Revolution* and Mark Steel's very funny and informative *Vive La Revolution* about the French Revolution. For a taste of the evils done by the US and colonial powers in Congo, watch *Lumumba*.

† W. E. B. DuBois's *Black Reconstruction in America* is one of the most

We have to recover our revolutionary history, not as dry lists of names and dates, but as conversations with our political ancestors about what to learn from their triumphs and failures. So rather than rattle off a few details from a number of revolutions, we're going to take a closer look at the most famous and infamous one of all.

The short version of the Russian Revolution that most of us learn goes something like this: In 1917, the Russian people were angry about being poor and drafted to die in World War I by their incompetent tsar (that's what Russian kings were called). This anger was skillfully manipulated by the Bolshevik Party and their crafty leader Vladimir Lenin in order to create a revolution that gave the Bolsheviks absolute power to impose their fanatical socialist ideals on the country, leading to decades of misery under Lenin's sidekick Joseph Stalin.

This story gets two things right: the angry people in the beginning and the misery under Stalin after the revolution was defeated. But there's some stuff in between—very interesting stuff in which millions of Russian workers, peasants, and soldiers formed the largest democratic bodies in history, created the beginnings of a new type of society the world had never seen, and inspired workers in dozens of countries to form their own Communist parties—that are left out of the picture.

What began as the closest thing we've seen to a worker-led society became an object lesson for generations of US schoolchildren for why socialism can't work. All this may have happened a century ago, but it's important for anyone interested in socialism in the twenty-first century to know what happened and what might have been.*

---

important US history books ever written because it undid the racist and once-dominant view that Reconstruction was a disaster of Black corruption. It's also really long. For a short history of reconstruction, Eric Foner wrote a book called, well, *A Short History of Reconstruction*.

* There are a million good books written about the Russian Revolution and a zillion—sorry, a shlazillion—bad ones. The most insightful and movingly written is Leon Trotsky's *History of the Russian Revolution*, but it's 1,200 pages and presumes you already know some of the history. For starters, there's China Mieville's *October*, or Amy Muldoon's informative two-part introduction to Trotsky's book at the website of the *International Socialist Review*.

Let's follow the advice of many an anticommunist over the years and go back to Russia.

In Soviet Russia

The first thing to understand about the Russian Revolution is that there was not one revolution but two: the overthrow of the tsar in February and the creation of a soviet government in October. The February Revolution was not planned by Lenin—or anybody else. It exploded mostly spontaneously after a strike of women clothing workers spread across the capital city—with the help of the Bolsheviks and other socialists—and snowballed into an unstoppable force that within days forced the tsar to step down and created a new provisional (or temporary) government.

The February Revolution had all the classic features of a revolution's initial days: unpredictability, a joyous disbelief that a regime that had been all-powerful for so long could be overthrown so easily, and a leading role played by working women.* The first provisional government was dominated by parties from the wealthy landowning and capitalist classes, which is also not unusual. After a tyrant is overthrown, the initial government to replace it often contains people who for the most part supported the old regime but now claim to have always been on the side of the people. At this early stage many of the people are okay with that. They are carried away by the beautiful unity that toppled the tyrant and still think it natural for those with the most money, status, and education to run society. In these early days different classes can celebrate together without taking up the inevitable question of who will be in charge of the store once everybody goes back to work. Factory workers and factory owners who will soon be at each other's throats can toast together the fall of the king.

But after a week or two of widespread public partying and hugging strangers in the street the way folks tend to do after they've over-

* Throughout history you know things are about to get real whenever working women start protesting because they are too burdened by daily responsibilities to have time for empty speeches.

thrown a thousand-year-old dictatorship, the people of Russia were confronted with the question of what to do next. The whole country agreed—or at least claimed to agree—that there should be a democratic government. But beyond that loomed huge disagreements. Poor peasants—the majority of the country—wanted land. Industrial workers and their families wanted a shorter workday and an end to food shortages. Wealthy businessmen and landowners, not surprisingly, had other ideas. Meanwhile, both peasants and workers wanted Russia to pull out of World War I, which had already killed more than 1.5 million Russian soldiers. But Russia's powerful allies England and France needed Russia to keep fighting, and the businessmen and landowners depended on those allies for loans and political support.

For the elites in charge of the provisional government, democracy meant having an elected government (someday at least—they kept putting off the elections) that would maintain the tsar's policies, most importantly continuing the war. In the US, we are very familiar with this version of democracy—the kind where no matter whom you elect the same powerful interests always remains in charge. But the provisional government's plans were challenged by new organizations created by the revolution called soviets. These were councils of elected representatives that started in the factories of the capital and then spread among workers, peasants, soldiers, students, women, neighborhoods, and villages. In the capital city these soviets controlled the factories that made weapons for the war, the post office, and railroads—and as the year went on, their influence spread across the country. Military officers on the front could not even have their orders carried out without the approval of the soldiers' council, which put a crimp in the army's go-to strategy of sending wave after wave of poor peasant soldiers to certain death.*

Since the soviets were performing many of the functions of government—in a radically more democratic way—the Bolsheviks

* Many Russian soldiers were sent into battle without boots—this is in freezing-ass Russia—or guns, which have also been known to be useful on the battlefield. But please remember that it's Lenin and the Bolsheviks who were the heartless tyrants.

argued that they could and should become the new government and begin the construction of a socialist society. Not surprisingly, Russia's upper classes weren't big fans of this plan, but neither were the two other socialist parties, which had a reformist approach that the revolution needed to limit itself to creating a democratic government led by capitalists, because economically backward Russia had a working class that was too small and underdeveloped to take power. Only many years later, they argued, would a socialist revolution be possible. The Bolsheviks agreed that it would be impossible for socialism to develop in Russia alone, but they believed that the example of a successful workers' revolution in Russia could inspire similar revolutions in countries like Germany, where greater economic resources and a larger and more powerful working class could make socialism a reality.

The Bolsheviks were a minority force in the soviets at the beginning of the revolution, but that changed as the year went on and the provisional government continued to find new excuses for not meeting the demands of workers and peasants, most of which began with "as soon as we win this war." Through months of stormy protests, strikes, peasant uprisings, and army mutinies, the Bolsheviks grew from a few thousand based among the most radical factory workers to an organization of hundreds of thousands based in many workplaces and throughout the army and navy. When in August a right-wing general named Kornilov tried to launch a coup and the hapless provisional government didn't know what to do, it was the Bolshevik-influenced soviets of railroad and telegraph workers who stopped him, as Bolshevik leader Leon Trotsky later described in his *History of the Russian Revolution*:

> The railroad workers in those days did their duty. In a mysterious way echelons [of Kornilov's troops] would find themselves moving on the wrong roads. Regiments would arrive in the wrong division, artillery would be sent up a blind alley, staffs would get out of communication with their units. All the big stations had their own Soviets, their railroad workers' and their military committees. The telegraphers kept them informed of all events, all movements, all

> changes. The telegraphers also held up the orders of Kornilov. It was in this atmosphere that the Kornilov echelons advanced—or what was worse, stood still.

By the fall, Bolsheviks had been elected to the majority of the citywide soviets in the capital city, and party leaders were publicly debating each other in newspaper columns over whether and how to take power from the official government. When they finally did in October, the move was so widely supported that there were almost no soldiers in the capital who defended the official government, although the fighting in other cities lasted for a few weeks.

While the majority of Russian workers supported the October Revolution, the more moderate socialist parties rejected it on the grounds that it was not democratic because it hadn't been elected, a detail they hadn't found objectionable in February when the tsar was overthrown without a vote. Their accusation that the October Revolution was a tyrannical turn against the "democratic" February revolution has been echoed by most historians, so it's worth a response.

Every revolution happens without a popular vote. If the change people are looking for could happen within the election process, there would be no need to revolt. Just as a revolution was necessary in February because a democracy couldn't be created under the tsar's monarchy, another one was necessary in October because soviets couldn't take power and create a far more democratic government under the direct control of the working masses while the provisional government controlled (or tried to control) the army, police, and other wings of the state. A revolution is usually initiated by a minority, but it can only succeed if that minority can win the support of the majority, which is what occurred both in February and in October.

Over the course of 1917 the Russian working class had, as Marx described, both changed the conditions of the country and changed itself through its creation of and participation in the soviets. Workers supported the October Revolution not because they were manipulated by the Bolshevik Party but because they came to agree with its strategies and theory through their own experience of power and self-organization.

What then happened after the October Revolution was the exact opposite of a small party seizing power for itself. The first acts of the new soviet government were directed toward giving workers control of the factories and peasants control of the land—not through strict government control but through their own actions. These decrees called on the soviets and other popular committees of workers and peasants to take over the land and factories themselves. The Bolsheviks were using their control of the government to create a new kind of state based on people taking power for themselves.

Within weeks, the soviet government had called for an immediate end to Russia's participation in the war and legalized divorce, abortion, and homosexuality—narrowly beating the United States on these progressive reforms by around fifty years or so.* It also declared that nations controlled by the tsar's empire had the right to declare independence, and embarrassed Russia's "democratic" allies England and France by publishing their secret plans to divide up the colonial territories of their enemies after the war.†

While all this was taking place in Russia, the revolutionary wave did indeed spread elsewhere, as the Bolsheviks had hoped. Two months after the October Revolution, Germany was shut down by a weeklong strike that called for immediate peace with Russia, in addition to raising German workers' own economic demands. A year later came a full revolution, which included the creation of German workers' soviets. But the German socialist movement was dominated

---

* Contrast the lightning pace of these changes to how long it takes to pass anything when Democrats have the government. Once when Barack Obama was president his spokesman was asked why it was taking three years just to end the military's "don't ask don't tell" policy toward gay soldiers. The response was that the president "has a lot on his plate." Slow eater, I guess.

† Sometimes I imagine what it must have been like to be in Russia for all this. Then I remember how when Donald Trump served some McDonald's in the White House, Washington insiders sniffed about *etiquette!* and *protocol!* like they were Effie from *The Hunger Games*. Let's just say it makes me wish even harder for a revolution because I would very much like certain people to see what a real "violation of norms" looks like.

by the same type of moderates who rejected the October Revolution in Russia. Like their Russian counterparts, the German moderates argued that the country wasn't ready for workers to take direct power. Unlike their Russian counterparts, they were able to use their authority in the new government to disband the soviets, repress the revolutionary workers, and murder the radical leaders Rosa Luxemburg and Karl Liebknecht. See, that's the democratic way to have a revolution.

There were more uprisings to come in Germany and elsewhere, but no successful revolutions, which made the eventual failure of the Russian Revolution inevitable, as the Bolsheviks knew. They had always said that socialism couldn't succeed if it was isolated in Russia—and that was before the country was wrecked by World War I and then invaded by foreign powers after the revolution. In the years after 1917, workers in Russian cities faced starvation, while peasants were furious that the new government they had fought for was now taking their bread to feed the workers.

As workers lost their strength and organization, real authority shifted from soviets to the bureaucracy of the Bolshevik government. Many peasants turned against the revolution and led uprisings that were suppressed. Leaders like Lenin and Trotsky publicly worried that the popular character of the revolution was deteriorating and urged government officials to maintain as much democratic culture as possible while waiting for new revolutions to break out in other countries and relieve Russia's isolation. But that was a holding pattern, not a strategy. It's a testament to the inspirational power of the revolution that, even during these troubled years in the 1920s, Russia saw artistic explosions in cinema and graphic design, breakthroughs in the study of psychology, and a sexual revolution that reached deep into the countryside.*

As it became clear the revolution wasn't going to quickly spread to other countries, there were sharp disagreements among leading Bolsheviks over how much to centralize power to prevent counterrevolution. Joseph Stalin emerged as the organizer of the most ruthless

* Don't worry. We'll come back to peasant sex in chapter 10.

current that pushed to create an autocracy rather than to wait to be overthrown by foreign armies and the old Russian ruling classes. Stalin maneuvered his way into a dictatorship that launched a historic reign of terror of slave labor camps, population transfers, and mass executions—each atrocity cynically hailed as a victory for the Russian working class. Every gain of the revolution was reversed: art and writing were rigorously censored, homosexuality and abortion were criminalized again, and women were told that being a good communist meant having lots of children for Mother Russia.

From that point on until its collapse in 1991, the Soviet Union's main contribution to the international working class was its brute military strength (minus the soldiers' councils, of course). Russia bore the brunt of casualties and fighting against Germany's Nazi regime in the Second World War and its vast troop levels and nuclear arsenal prevented the US and its Western European allies from dominating every region of the post-war world. This was especially important during the wave of independence movements in former colonies across Africa and Asia in the mid-twentieth century—the most important global freedom movement in modern history. But while some of these new countries called themselves Marxist and adopted aspects of Russia's state-run economic model, many also emulated its lack of democracy, giving more ammunition to socialism's critics.

Stalin, a longtime dedicated Bolshevik turned ruthless tyrant, is the poster child for the commonsense idea that power inevitably corrupts. But the claim that a revolution that saw tens of millions participating in mass soviet democracy became a monstrous dictatorship because of one man's ruthless thirst for power is a nursery-rhyme version of history, like saying the American Revolution succeeded because George Washington was so honest about chopping down that cherry tree.

The defeat from within of the Soviet Union's democratic and emancipating potential was a decade-long process. The soviets stopped functioning in conditions of war and mass poverty and the Bolshevik Party was left in charge of a state presiding over a devastated economy. As the party had to make more and more emergency decisions—often with the fate of the revolution on the line—the revolutionary dynamic of the people fighting for their own liberation completely shifted to a small number of ex-revolutionaries fighting for their own position as the leaders of the country. Bolshevik leaders faced a series of sharp conflicts with no good options. The bad choices of some were understandable, others unforgivable. But it was the bleak context of a revolution inside a devastated country that made the consequences of these decisions so disastrous.

The lesson we're meant to take from the Russian Revolution is that power always corrupts and everyday people who join revolutions are being duped by one or another group of elites. People have good reason to be suspicious that socialists intend to simply use workers as an army to overturn capitalism and then turn on them once in power. History is filled with examples of revolutions that end with the masses being betrayed by the leaders they put into power. In fact, the charge that many a good USA patriot has leveled at the Bolsheviks—that they used the revolutionary masses for their own gain—applies far more accurately to his revered Founding Fathers than to Lenin and Trotsky.

The American Revolution wasn't fought in the name of Indigenous people, women, or African Americans, but it did mobilize poor farmers to fight and die to kick out the British and establish a republic that saw all white men as being equal. Just three years after the war ended, Daniel Shays led an armed protest of some of those Massachusetts farmers and war veterans who were being thrown into jail for being unable to make debt payments to wealthy Boston bankers. The response to Shays' Rebellion from the leaders of the revolutionary new country was to create a new constitution with a stronger central government that could more ruthlessly put down future rebellions of the poor.

The Bolsheviks have been demonized for the past hundred years because, unlike the leaders of the American Revolution, they actually tried to fulfill their radical promises, pushing past the initial stage of a new elite taking control to a more radical transformation of society in which power really was in the hands of the masses of people. Their ultimate failure was a tragic confirmation of the core Marxist conviction that socialism can only be created by a strong working class.

History Is a Teacher, Not an Instruction Manual

For over half a century after the Bolshevik revolution, workers' councils reappeared in a number of revolutionary situations: Spain in 1936, Hungary in 1956, Chile in 1972, Iran in 1978, Poland in 1981. As in Russia, the existence of these councils created the potential for a situation known as dual power, in which the normal authority of government is challenged—although not always consciously—by these new workers' organizations. These situations are unstable and cannot last for very long. The Bolsheviks used the eight months of dual power to organize support for the soviets to take over. No major party in these later revolutions was willing or able to do the same, and in each case the government was able to take back control, disband the councils, and roll back the revolution.*

Then beginning in the 1970s came a long global period of increasing wealth inequality and declining working-class power in many parts of the world—especially in the United States. This era is often called neoliberalism, a long and awful word for a long and awful time in history that we may or may not still be trapped inside.† There have been many revolutions and near-revolutions over recent decades—

---

* One reason these uprisings were unable to match the success of the Russian Revolution was, ironically, the Russian Revolution. The Bolsheviks' unique achievements won the loyalty of radical working-class parties around the world. Stalin and his successors abused that loyalty to turn those parties away from revolution and toward acting like a "responsible opposition" that would encourage their governments to build alliances with Russia.

† One way to define neoliberalism is as a set of policies that weaken unions and government social programs in favor of "free trade" and "free market" policies. The political scientist Wendy Brown defines it more expansively as an all-encompassing transformation of political, social, and cultural life into a bleak set of business-consumer interactions. When I'm feeling lazy, I just describe neoliberalism as what capitalism looks like when our side is getting its ass kicked.

from the movement that overthrew apartheid in South Africa to the many South American protests and street mobilizations that both brought down reactionary governments and defended the ensuing "Pink Tide" governments from being overthrown. The Arab Spring of 2011 was the most dramatic revolutionary moment of this era, both in its thrilling spread across North Africa and the Middle East and in its moving public scenes of liberation and discovery. Here is a *New York Times* report from Yemen in June of that magical year:

> In the sprawling tent city outside Sana University, rival tribesmen have forsworn their vendettas to sit, eat and dance together. College students talk to Zaydi rebels from the north and discover they are not, in fact, the devils portrayed in government newspapers. Women who have spent their lives indoors give impassioned speeches to amazed crowds. Four daily newspapers are now published in "Change Square," as it is called, and about 20 weeklies.

But in a neoliberal era that has been marked by the weakening of unions around the world, strikes and workers' organizations have mainly played secondary roles in the revolutions that have taken place, which has made them weaker and more easily defeated.* There have been no workers councils in the last forty years, no situations of dual power, and so it's been less clear what power revolutions still have.

"What is a revolution?" asked the anarchist writer David Graeber in 2013 as the Arab Spring revolutions were in retreat:

> We used to think we knew. Revolutions were seizures of power by popular forces aiming to transform the very nature of the political, social, and economic system in the country in which the revolution took place, usually according to some visionary dream of a just society. Nowadays, we live in an age when, if rebel armies do come sweeping into a city, or mass uprisings overthrow a dictator, it's unlikely to have any such implications; when profound social transformation does occur—as with, say, the rise of feminism—it's likely to take an entirely different form.

* It's not a coincidence that the only Arab Spring revolution to avoid rollback was in Tunisia where the union federation played a central role.

It's an accurate description of what political change has and hasn't looked like during many of our lifetimes. Most of the far-reaching and radical changes we've experienced, what Graeber called "planetwide transformations of common sense," haven't come from regime changes but, like feminism, from a not-quite-definable combination of protests, personal decisions, transformative art, radical manifestos, and viral moments.

Socialist revolution based on the dual power model of working-class power hasn't been on the agenda for decades and doesn't appear to be returning anytime soon. But it's as important as ever to have a revolutionary understanding of the world, to recognize the danger and power of the plates shifting underneath us. Yes, it's easier to imagine the end of the world than the end of capitalism, but the fight to save the world can open up new possibilities to create a better one.

Rosa Luxemburg wrote *Reform or Revolution* a century ago to argue against some of the earliest versions of reformist socialism. But the book's title shouldn't be taken out of that context to create a false choice. The path to socialism requires reforms *and* revolutions: the more victories we win that strengthen working-class power through unions, wealth redistribution, and racial and gender equality, the stronger and more organized our side can be in a revolution—which is a good thing since those victories will also increase the likelihood that we'll need a revolution to overcome the coups and civil wars coming our way.

Reforms and revolutions don't always occur in that order. The Bolsheviks expected a democratic revolution to topple the tsar and establish a system in which workers could better fight for more reforms until a future socialist revolution. That's not how things worked out in Russia, but perhaps one day we'll say that's what happened in South Africa. There, a political revolution in the 1990s overturned apartheid but left in place a system of vast economic inequality and corruption. Working-class Black South Africans have used the freedoms won in the victory over apartheid to build some of the world's most powerful social movements, which has made the country a hotspot of protest for most of the last three decades.

The US has already seen two revolutions—the first overthrew King George and the second overthrew slavery—and our biggest reforms like Social Security and the Civil Rights Act have been won during periods of general strikes and mass upheavals in the 1930s and 1960s. Since then our political system has become increasingly stifled by corporate money, Republican gerrymandering, and Democrats' cooptation of movements for change. Is it that farfetched to speculate that it might take revolutionary upheavals that destroy corrupt institutions like the Senate, Supreme Court, and two-party system—just to enable future struggles for commonsense reforms like free child care and a shift to renewable energy?

The fight for reforms can strengthen radical forces, but they also strengthen the reactionary forces of backlash, as we've seen in the wake of every wave of Black Lives Matter struggle. At the same time, strong movements for reforms by necessity end up creating durable organizations with leaders who sometimes no longer want to take risks that might jeopardize their careers. Mutual aid networks can become nonprofit organizations reluctant to alienate wealthy donors; unions can become more focused on partnering with employers to preserve jobs than challenging them for control over their pay and conditions; socialist parties worried about losing seats in government can retreat from principled positions against policing or war. The challenge then is that protest movements can lead to an enraged right-wing reaction just as our side is becoming more cautious. That's a dangerous combination.

Radicals develop different strategies to help keep the daily fight for reforms connected with our longer term aims of revolutionary change. Some aim for "non-reformist reforms" that not only win some things today but structurally change capitalism in ways that strengthen our ability to win more tomorrow. Medicare for All, for example, would obviously be a life-saving victory in its own right, but it would also allow workers to better push for higher wages and better conditions because they would no longer be constantly defending their insufficient health benefits.

Police and prison abolitionism is usually thought of as an analysis, but it's also a revolutionary strategy toward reforms. Abolitionists certainly reject reforms such as body cameras and bias training that keep power in control of repressive state agencies (and in fact often only increase their budgets). But they strongly support even the smallest measures that can reduce the funding and power of police and prisons—while organizing for community-based solutions to the problems that these institutions are supposedly meant to address. In this way, the abolition movement builds connections among hundreds of local struggles—banning the use of solitary confinement, getting a cop with a record of violence fired, increasing jobs programs for poor youth—while helping activists maintain a vision for the more transformative goal of a society that builds public safety through grassroots democratic participation rather than government repression.

Whatever our framework, however, there's no exact formula for avoiding the pitfalls of reformism on one side and ultra-radical impotence on the other. We're all going to make lot of mistakes—sometimes by making too many compromises, other times by making too few. What's more important is being able to admit when we're wrong and to keep looking for connections between where we are today and where we want to be tomorrow.

While revolutionaries like George Washington and Alexander Hamilton used grand rhetoric to mask the goal of transferring power from one group of rich guys to another, socialists really are trying to change the entire social order and should be modest about how much of that change we can control. Whatever slogans our future revolutions adopt, let's also keep in mind the old Yiddish one, "*Mann Tracht, Un Gott Lacht*": Man plans, and God laughs.

But of course, we still have to plan, and we still need the seizures of power and visionary dreams—even as we understand why Graeber views them skeptically. Workers' councils may not be on the visible horizon but irreversible temperature increases sure are, and possibly right-wing coups, martial law, and new forms of fascism. On the other side of the ledger we have globally resurgent movements for feminism, Indigenous rights, and Black lives, a revitalized socialist movement in the US, a young generation that is way more radical than its predecessors, and a working class that is still weak in terms of union organization but beginning to break out of decades of demoralization.

The role of revolutionaries is not so much to create revolutions as to prepare for them, and that's hard because there are no guarantees about when they'll arrive. What we do know is that the next one will happen sooner than those in power claim—which is never again. In the meantime, there are the small and not-so-small struggles that capitalism makes inevitable: picket lines and protests against police violence, high school walkouts and hunger strikes. It is in these fights that new revolutionaries are forged, and it is the goal of socialists to bring them together into effective organizations.

These future socialist parties will look different from the Bolsheviks—although in the US they'll probably still be accused of being funded by Russia—and our revolutions might barely resemble theirs. But what we will hopefully have in common is the belief in the capacity of ordinary people to create a better society, and the courage, desire, and intelligence to recognize those rare moments when that's a possibility, and seize them for all they're worth.

9.

WAIT, IS THIS COMMUNISM?

I have a confession to make. You've been a terrific reader, putting up with my weak metaphors and Dad jokes in order to just learn a little more about socialism. Which only makes it harder for me to admit that I've been misleading you this whole time. Despite its title, this thing I've been describing for the last eight chapters isn't socialism. It might actually be communism. Wait no, maybe it's post-Trotskyist neo-Draperian Marxism. I made that last one up, but my point is that there are many different streams of thought in the socialist wilderness. Different strategies have emerged out of the various circumstances that socialists have encountered through history, and out of these strategies have grown entirely different theories about what socialism is and how we get there.

What I've been describing, a revolutionary project based on the potential of the working class to overthrow capitalism and create a classless society, has generally been known as Marxism.* But I can't even claim that this book represents all Marxists, who disagree with one another (quite loudly) over any number of subjects. Take the "Russia question," which has been as much of a touchstone for the left as the *Twilight* movies were for a generation of teenage girls, only if Edward had his henchmen stab Jacob with an ice pick and liquidate

* There's an irony to people who agree with Marx calling themselves "Marxists"—but you know that already because you read the footnote in chapter 4 about Marx saying that he's not a Marxist. By the way, do you know that some people don't bother coming down here to read these? Rude, right? Don't tell them I said this, but you're my favorite reader.

his entire family. That's what Joseph Stalin did to Leon Trotsky, who had become the leader of the forces opposed to Stalin's destruction of the Russian Revolution. For decades after, the radical left was bitterly divided between "Stalinists" and "Trotskyists." As you can probably tell by now, I'm on Team Leon.*

Russia is just one of the many points of disagreement among socialists. Other perennial debate topics include "Reform versus Revolution," "Race versus Class," and "Sellout versus Loser," each of which raise rich questions that can advance our movement through thoughtful discussion but more often are fodder for useless Twitter fights that get a few people more followers while making the rest of us depressed. The left is notorious for our endless arguments, although I find that critique a little rich coming from those who breathlessly follow the daily screaming matches in the Capitol between the party for endless war and oil drilling and the party for endless war and even more oil drilling. Compared to that racket, arguments among socialists are far more profound—at least for those who can follow what's going on.

Many people discover socialism where they find everything else, on the internet—that dizzying space of random facts, purposeful lies, community building, and competitive status seeking. They eagerly search for basic information about socialist ideas while having fun picking up the inside jokes and sectarian insults of burned-out veterans. They denounce the invasion of Ukraine, and then post Stalin memes to own the libs. And through it all, they may or may not get a straight answer to their most basic questions.

Sometimes that's because there is no simple answer. Take one of the most common questions: what's the difference between socialism and communism? Early socialists used the two words almost interchangeably. In some writings, Marx and Engels used *socialism* to refer

---

* This joke is from the first edition, when I could not have predicted that *Twilight* would have less currency with the online youth than Stalin and Trotsky. I like the change, but kids should be required to at least watch the baseball scene from the first movie so that they can appreciate the hell their elders lived through.

to a transition period after a working-class revolution, and *communism* to refer to a later era when class inequality had been fully eliminated. But this distinction didn't stop them from using both words to label their ideas, as in the titles of their two most popular books: *The Communist Manifesto* and *Socialism: Utopian and Scientific*.

But later events would lead Marxists to divide themselves into two camps, and *socialism* became the label for mainly Western European governments with a strong welfare state, while *communism* was used to describe regimes in poorer parts of the world that resisted US domination through highly centralized one-party regimes that were usually allied with the Soviet Union. Neither of the models—which could more accurately be named *parliamentary socialism* and *state socialism*—had much to do with the original understanding of socialism/communism. And thus we have a problem: you ask a basic question about the difference between socialism and communism, I respond with a long, winding speech about how actually that's the wrong question, you tune me out and go back to searching Bernie memes.

There's no getting around the fact that it's hard to understand the important differences on the left without some knowledge of their roots in key historical events. Socialists are also often ridiculed for being obsessed with history and nursing ancient grudges. That second point is well taken, but I stand by the need to know our past. A close study of history is the essence of archaeology, evolutionary biology, and many other fields of human knowledge. New activists are often more eager to organize protests than learn about past ones, but most soon learn that they aren't the first generation trying to change the world, and they eventually come to identify with one or more of the distinct strains of socialism bequeathed to us by previous generations.

Welcome to the Family!

There have been many philosophies throughout history that would be considered socialist today, from the ideas that governed a number of Indigenous societies over hundreds of years to the anti-imperialist and egalitarian teachings of that radical Palestinian Jew, Jesus

Christ. Modern socialism started in Europe in reaction to the emergence of capitalism, and as capitalism spread around the world so did socialist opposition.*

Almost immediately, different strategies and currents of thought began to emerge, from Marx and Engels's break from utopian socialists to the divisions that emerged soon after between Marx's followers and anarchists like Pierre-Joseph Proudhon and Mikhail Bakunin. Anarchism and socialism are anticapitalist siblings, with all the close bonds and bitter rivalries that implies. Anarchism has as many variations as socialism but is generally characterized by its opposition to all forms of state power—including representative democracies—and its suspicion of large-scale political parties.†

As the socialist parties inspired by Marx grew, they became host to radical and conservative tendencies, with the moderates increasingly focused on building broad electoral parties and following the lead of more conservative union leaders, both of which could lead to their echoing the colonial and racist prejudices of the day.‡ These tensions came to a boil with the revolutionary wave that swept across Russia, Germany, and most of Europe almost a hundred years

---

* Some have argued that Marxism is inherently Eurocentric—and at times racist—because of these historical origins. I believe its disproportionate popularity among non-white peoples around the world disproves this criticism, but some of these critiques have important insights into some of the blind spots and faulty assumptions of many pioneering Marxists. See for example the great Palestinian writer Edward Said's *Orientalism* and Cedric Robinson's *Black Marxism*.

† This orientation in my opinion limits anarchism's ability to pose an effective challenge to capitalism, but it has also helped anarchists make critical contributions to social movements through their emphasis on direct democracy, community building, and grassroots protest.

‡ If you're interested in a deep dive into the good, bad, and ugly about racism and the early US socialist movement—and the history of some incredible and overlooked early Black socialists—check out Paul Heideman's *Class Struggle and the Color Line: American Socialism and the Race Question: 1900–1930*. Or listen to the interview we did with Paul on my old podcast *Better Off Red* (episode 6).

ago.* While most of the socialist movement initially cheered the revolution against the hated tsar, the Bolsheviks' strategies and organizational model sharpened long-existing divisions among socialists, and led to the emergence around the world of competing socialist and communist parties.

The latter came together in an international body of communist parties called the Comintern, which came under strict Bolshevik control as the Russian party (and its revolution) became more autocratic.† On the other side of the socialist divide were the socialist parties, which claimed to support the overthrow of capitalism by the working class but increasingly argued that this would occur not through revolutionary upheavals but via gradual implementation from elected governments—a framework that would become known as social democracy.

As world capitalism's crisis deepened with the Great Depression and World War II, many European social democratic parties won national elections and had the chance to test out their theory of slow and steady socialist transformation. They enacted programs of free health care and higher education (as did many non-socialist governments in this period) which represented major progress but didn't challenge the overall authority of the capitalist class to run the economy based on profit. On the rare occasions they tried to go further and take public ownership of major companies, such as in France in the 1980s, capitalists forced them to back down with threats to sabotage the economy, which would gravely hurt their chances in the next election.

These confrontations were the exception, however, and as capitalists and social democrats learned how to coexist—and even get along—social democracy moved away from even mild reformism. Starting in the 1990s, most of these parties distanced themselves from

* Apologies to Mexico and Ireland, which are the often overlooked first revolutions of that era. Come to think of it, double apologies for what my country has done to St. Patrick's Day and Cinco de Mayo.

† *Comintern,* which came from "communist international," was a typical linguistic creation of Russian communists, who got as excited about combining words as preteens coming up with "ship names" for all the middle school couples. *Agitprop! Proletkult!* Omigod this is so fun, Vladlena!

their roots in the labor movement and adopted the corporate-funded model and principle-free politics of the Democratic Party. It's no coincidence that European politics has started to look more like the US, with many working-class people alienated from politics and some attracted to far-right scapegoating of immigrants and Muslims.

While social democracy was starting down its rightward course, the still powerful Communist parties, which organized strong unions and protests but tolerated little dissent and unquestioningly supported Stalin's regime, faced a series of defections from scattered groups of Trotskyists, Black radicals, and others who opposed the Soviet Union's turn toward dictatorship and maintained that socialism must be both revolutionary *and* democratic. As the world learned about the slave labor camps, mass executions, and other horrors of Stalinism, Russia's revolutionary prestige faded, and the next generation found its inspiration in China, Cuba, and the tremendous revolutionary tide that swept across Africa, Asia, and Latin America in the mid-twentieth century.

The Chinese Revolution emerged from a remarkable shift in strategy, one that changed millions of people's ideas of where socialism could come from—and maybe what it even means. The Chinese Communist Party had been one of the world's largest revolutionary working-class organizations, but in the 1920s it was massacred and suppressed following a failed revolution. Under Mao Zedong, the remaining party members retreated from the cities into the countryside and remade themselves into a peasant army that over the next twenty years would resist Japanese occupation and win power from China's corrupt and discredited ruling elites. In an effort to quickly build a strong military and industrial base, Mao emulated Russia's most brutal years under Stalin. Despite the resulting famines and hardships, China for a time appeared to offer a way to resist imperialism and build socialism in countries with more peasants than workers—and Maoism continues to inspire mass resistance movements in countries like India and the Philippines.

Socialist aims guided many of the revolutions that broke out across the colonized and semi-colonized world, with many different results.

Ho Chi Minh's Communist Party won Vietnam's independence from France and then resisted a decade of all-out American war. Under Kwame Nkrumah, Ghana built international organizations to promote pan-African unity and for newly independent countries to have the freedom to not align with either the US or Russia. Cuba established impressive national literacy and public health in the face of a crippling US embargo. These and many other revolutions and decolonization struggles created a conventional wisdom in the mid-twentieth century that progressive and even radical change was something to be expected. That's something we dearly miss today. But because most of them took place in countries where the working class was small and the threat of coups or foreign intervention was high, they often reinforced the legacy of Stalin and Mao that socialism was about centralized economic and military planning at the expense of democracy. There were exceptions. The Bolivian Revolution of 1952 was led by miners, and the Hungarian Revolution of 1956 (against the Russia-backed "communist" government!) saw the growth of workers' councils similar to soviets. But it was a sign of the times that neither of these revolutions were nearly as influential on the left as those in Cuba and China.*

And so it came to pass that Marxism was generally seen as having two options: the reformism of social democracy on one side, and one-party "people's" dictatorships on the other. This division was—and still is—commonly expressed as *socialism* versus *communism*, which distorts the meaning of not one word but two. Is this book a socialist book or a communist book? By the definitions they have come to acquire, it's neither. But by their original definitions, which I find more useful, it's both. I use socialism because that word is less scary to some potential readers. If that changes, I'll have no problem renaming it *Communism . . . Come On!*

By the end of the twentieth century, the Soviet Union had collapsed, China still called itself communist while being the world's

* What you just read was an incredibly—some might say criminally—condensed history of nearly two centuries of socialism. You can find a much more thorough introduction to all of this in Bhaskar Sunkara's *The Socialist Manifesto.*

fastest growing capitalist economy, and Europe's social democrats had dropped any pretense of working toward a socialist transformation. It was a tough time for many on the left but also the beginning of a global period of experimentation, kicked off by the 1994 Zapatista uprising in southern Mexico that created (and has maintained) government-free "autonomous" towns and popular assemblies. The Zapatistas demonstrated the effectiveness and inspiration of non-hierarchical organizing models and direct democracy in public spaces, and their strategies would come to influence abolitionists, Occupy and Black Lives Matter activists, and many organizers in the Arab Spring. The Zapatistas were also an early example of the increasing interplay of socialist, anarchist, and Indigenous organizing models that would play a large role in many of the movements that created South America's "Pink Tide."

Those attempts by radicals in Venezuela, Ecuador, Bolivia, and Brazil to advance socialism through elected governments backed by social movements had only limited success, as we've seen. But that limited success, combined with the inability of Occupy and other protest movements to win lasting change, inspired a revival of radical socialist electoral campaigns via Bernie Sanders in the US, Jeremy Corbyn in Britain, and new parties like Podemos in Spain and SYRIZA in Greece. These attempts, though so far unsuccessful, have at least put the idea of socialist governments back into the public imagination.

In the US, the Sanders campaigns also helped turn the tiny Democratic Socialists of America into the largest socialist party the US has seen since the heyday of the Socialist and Communist Parties in the early twentieth century. "Democratic socialism" means different things to different people (are you surprised at this point?). But it generally refers to ideas first developed in the 1970s by European radicals like Ralph Miliband and Nicholas Poulanzas, who argued that socialism in wealthy capitalist countries would have to be achieved through electoral campaigns backed by strikes and powerful social protests.

The growth of DSA, combined with historic levels of Black radical protest, an Indigenous-led global environmental movement, and a left that is increasingly led by people who are queer, trans, and women of color, makes for some exciting times for socialists. And yet, we're also still getting our asses kicked. There's an exciting new socialist left emerging, but we're confronting all the old questions of how to win power against capitalist opposition—and now we're doing it under the horrible new conditions of climate catastrophe and social media mind-manipulation. We're going to have to shake up the socialist snow globe and sprinkle together the best ideas and practices from our many different radical traditions. It will take a new generation exploring socialism with fresh eyes to show us the way.

Please hurry.

What's in a Name?

This is an introductory book, so I've tried to be fair to as many different socialist tendencies as possible without revealing too many of my own biases. But since I'm failing miserably, let me put my cards on the table.

I come out of the relatively tiny Trotskyist movement, which has kept chugging along through the decades, trying to maintain what we viewed as the true spirit of Marxism, with its emphasis on working-class democratic self-rule. The American Trotskyist Hal Draper summarized this view in *The Two Souls of Socialism*, which argued that both social democracy and Stalinism, different as they are, were both forms of "socialism from above"—one calling for workers to be liberated by benevolent socialists in parliament, the other by benevolent socialists in Red Army tanks:

> There have always been different "kinds of socialism," and they have customarily been divided into reformist or revolutionary, peaceful or violent, democratic or authoritarian, etc. These divisions exist, but the underlying division is something else. Throughout the history of socialist movements and ideas, the fundamental divide is between socialism-from-above and socialism-from-below.
>
> What unites the many different forms of socialism-from-above is the conception that socialism must be handed down to the grateful masses in one form or another, by a ruling elite which is not subject to their control in fact. The heart of socialism-from-be-

> low is its view that socialism can be realized only through the self-emancipation of activized masses "from below" in a struggle to take charge of their own destiny as actors (not merely subjects) on the stage of history. "The emancipation of the working classes must be conquered by the working classes themselves"; this is the first sentence in the rules written for the First International by Marx, and this is the first principle of his life work.

It's my inner Trotskyist that makes it difficult for me to answer questions about the difference between socialism and communism. First, I have to clarify that what you might think is socialism (Sweden) and what you might think is communism (Cuba) aren't really either, and by the time I get to answering your question, you've walked away. Perhaps this is why many Trotskyist groups have often struggled to attract more than small numbers of intellectuals.* It's usually not a great idea to resist the changing definitions of words. You sound like the old guy complaining about all the people these days who say *literally* when they mean the opposite. More problematically, it's not a great look for Trotskyists to quote dead white European socialists in an effort to prove why dozens of attempts to move toward socialism outside of Europe don't qualify as "real" socialism.

On the other hand, ever since the collapse of the Russian Revolution into Stalin's dictatorship, it has been disastrous for socialists to go along with the insistence of dictators that their oppressive societies be labeled communist or socialist. People have the right to tell you what name to call them. Governments do not. Today, few people look at China or North Korea as socialist role models, but there remains among some socialists an unhealthy habit of whitewashing the problems of any government that calls itself socialist or speaks against US foreign policy—even when ordinary people in those countries are taking to the streets in opposition. Socialists inside the US have a responsibility to build opposition to our own government's invasions and financial domination of people around the world. But building

* My old comrades are going to kill me if I don't mention that there have also been important exceptions where Trotskyists have led major strikes and protest movements—and also that Trotskyists are super sexy.

international solidarity also involves listening to and amplifying the voices of those people, including when they have legitimate grievances against their own governments. We should always be skeptical of US propaganda, but that skepticism crosses into conspiracy theory when it dismisses millions of protesters in countries like Iran and Syria as mere puppets of US intelligence agencies. Socialists who support repressive governments simply because the US opposes them fail to achieve the internationalism they are aiming for. Instead, they are strangely provincial, looking at the world only from the perspective of the US government (so that they can oppose it) rather than that of ordinary people across the globe.

Fighting to maintain socialism's meaning as a democratic society based on workers power is about keeping our aims from being distorted by governments looking to exaggerate their achievements or justify their crimes. It's also about keeping our sights on what this is all for. There are a number of socialist parties that currently hold office, but there are no socialist countries—not because socialism is a paradise that's impossible to achieve but because it requires a level of organization and power among the working class and other oppressed members of society that we haven't yet managed to reach.

With all these debates, some may think this means it's not helpful to identify with any one label that they fear could restrict their uniquely individual worldview. But deciding to be a socialist or anarchist doesn't limit your ideas. It gives them more structure, which actually helps you think for yourself in a society dominated by the ideas of capitalism. Most activists who reject all "isms" are deluding themselves that they are free thinkers when in fact they are limited thinkers, avoiding a systematic assessment of the "ism" that shapes every aspect of our lives and thoughts. It's an illusion shared by COVID skeptics who think "doing their own research" means getting duped by a YouTube con artist, or "independent" voters who simply vote by alternating between the same lousy Democrats and Republicans.

Leftists who view themselves as political independents are usually unknowingly followers of liberalism, which can encompass the opinions of a wide range of people—from immigrants' rights activists to the Democrats who deport them. Liberalism is a default category. You don't have to make a decision to be a liberal—that's just what anyone who isn't conservative is called. But liberalism and conservatism both start from the proposition that capitalism is the best possible system—they differ in that liberalism thinks its problems should be reformed while conservatives fear the instability that comes with any form of change. Unlike liberalism, socialism must be a conscious choice: a rejection of the idea that humanity can't do better than capitalism. That's why identifying as a socialist doesn't limit your intellectual horizons but frees them.

Until recently, many would-be socialists argued that we should stop using a name with so much historical baggage. Isn't what we call ourselves less important than what we do, like supporting strikes and fighting deportations? Sure, but strikes and deportations have root causes in capitalism, and avoiding words like *socialism* means that we're not educating new activists about these root causes—or pointing a way forward to how we can ultimately live in a world free of all exploitation and national borders.

Now we're facing the opposite problem. Socialism isn't so radical at all, you'll hear. It's really just a reasonable mixture of communism and capitalism. Hell, we already have socialism in the form of government-run post offices, fire stations, and highways. Some of the people making these arguments think they are helping our movement by making the dreaded S-word less scary to mainstream voters. Others are consciously trying to steer us away from radical change. But at a time when the status quo is miserable and capitalism is destroying the only planet we have to live on, it's a terrible strategy to point at the crumbling world and say, "I'm not sure if you realized it, but actually, this is socialism!"

It's common sense among many activists that the best way to win influence is to be as broad and inclusive as possible to gain more people. But for that influence to mean anything, it has to be based on some sharp and specific ideas that point a definite way forward. The socialism (or communism!) presented in this book is more far-reaching than a slightly improved version of capitalism.

The bad news about this version of socialism is that the majority class around the world has to learn through its own painful struggles how to become the masters of society, which is a lot harder to accomplish than changing a few laws or even the whole government. The good news is that if the majority class around the world learns through its own painful struggles how to become the masters of society, it will be a lot harder to undo by changing a few laws or even the whole government.

PART IV

THE BEGINNING

2040: A HOT DAY IN QUEENS

You sit up in bed, feel the sweat on your legs, and whisper a curse. It's still dark out, but there's no point going back to bed. J, of course, is snoring peacefully away. How lovely it must be to sleep through the heat: not only are you well rested but you can be a perfect little socialist citizen who never turns on the emergency air conditioner.

Sleeping in an apartment built for a different climate is like sunbathing in a parka. When you stay over with friends in the Bronx, the difference is unbelievable. Why is it taking so freaking long to retrofit Queens buildings with better insulation and ventilation? Okay fine, you know why—your dad is in construction, and he tells you how much work it takes, and it's fine that the Bronx gets first priority because of poverty reparations. But if they start working on Brooklyn before Queens, you're going to stab somebody.

It's just wrong to be awake so early on a Late Day, especially after the battle you all had to wage yesterday to keep it. Ever since the midtown rooftop groves reported their avocados were starting to bear fruit, things have been a little crazy at Amazon—at least the Nile Center that handles food distribution. With all the late changes to grocery orders flooding in across Queens, Algee calculated that the late shift should come in the next day at the usual 9 a.m. instead of 11—and so of course that's what Douglas proposed.

Douglas is nice, but you don't like the way they run things when it's their turn in the monthly rotation as center manager. Their view is that schedules and assignments should be completely dictated by the recommendations of the Amazon algorithm.

"After all," they say, "Algee processes all the food requests, dietary health reports, and worker schedule requests. If you want, we can vote to bring a complaint to the next Algee Committee meeting and propose that our schedules weigh more heavily in the next upgrade. But that's not 'til next week, so we have to come in early tomorrow. Come on, comrades, this is socialism!"

Maybe you all would have grumbled and let it go if Douglas hadn't added that last line. Instead, they got an earful:

"Let me get this straight, Doug: socialism is mandatory overtime so that bougie comrades can have some avocado toast?"

"Or maybe the boss thinks it means doing whatever a computer tells us to do."

"Hey, Dougie, socialism is about people being able to make their own decisions!"

It started getting nasty, but the conversation took a turn when Nassir piped up to argue that humans can't just do whatever they want, and that we're in this mess because we stopped respecting plants and animals and non-living relations like rivers and mountains. Then someone else asked if a complex computer system like Algee is also part of nature. Suddenly there was talk about having a Friday discussion about artificial intelligence and the carbon-based lifeform binary—until people saw the pained look on Douglas's face because the center was falling way off schedule for the dinner sort. It was quickly decided to put off the conversation until Friday, and then everyone busted their asses to catch up and still get out by four. And there was no further mention of reporting early the next day.

So yes, you've earned the right to sleep in this morning, you think, as you defiantly turn on the emergency AC and silently dare J to wake up and criticize you for being selfish. The screen flashes on to warn you that New York City only has twenty million AC hours for the rest of the year. You press Confirm, and begin the ten-minute "cooling off period" (cruel irony, comrades) until you can hit Confirm again and finally feel some glorious air conditioning.

Will you get asked about this by someone on your neighborhood's energy usage committee? Probably. Will that be awkward for J since they're a member of that committee? Definitely. Screw it, you almost say out loud, as you enviously watch them sleep. Maybe they should care less about their public reputation and more about your sleep needs. Or how about trying to get you back on the AC Health Exemption list? Not being able to sleep on Late Day doesn't qualify but maybe it should.

You were on the exemption list when your mom died from COVID-27 and you couldn't get out of bed for what ended up being almost a month. This is when you were working earlies at a coffee shop, slinging coffee and oatmeal, and running 7 a.m. Sudoku tournaments for older people—mainly immigrants who had been pouring into Queens to reunite with their kids and grandkids, usually for a few months, sometimes for good. A lot of younger people were doing the same thing in reverse, arranging switches on the old Airbnb website so they could live in Nepal and Ghana with extended families they had barely known.

The Sudoku job was created after a study about the benefits of intergenerational relationships. You were a little nervous at first since you never even met your own grandparents, but you enjoyed hearing stories of 1990s life in the Philippines, Colombia, and Bangladesh. Until that awful day when you realized you were never going to hear any more Guatemala stories from your mom.

J is the one who answered when you called out of work. You'd only been coworkers for a few weeks, but they came over right away and took care of AC Exemption, as well as funeral arrangements, family counseling, neighborhood grocery delivery, everything. When the social worker from your mom's hospice came by an hour later, there's was nothing left for her to do except give you the wonderful advice to "snag whoever it was that took care of all this. That comrade is a keeper."

Yes, they are, and maybe they never should have gotten a spoiled jerk like you on the Exemption List in the first place when your mom died . . . five years ago today. Now you know why you're awake and in such a sour mood. With a sigh, you turn off the AC, make some coffee, take a cold shower, and kiss J on the head before heading over to meet your dad at the gravesite.

* * *

You love cemeteries, obviously. What's not to love? The riot of vibrant sculptures created by artists working with grieving loved ones; rolling hills of grass and wildflowers tended by landscapers trained in grief counseling (or grief counselors trained in landscaping); picnic grounds stocked with pizza, mac and cheese, and other comfort foods; jungle gyms for kids (mostly) to run around and adults to look over at them and be reminded of life amid all the death.

But none of this is why you're taking your time this morning, stopping at various strangers' sites to pick up the gray tablets and scroll through the pictures and eulogies. You're stalling before you have to confront the empty space that is still your mom's site—and make up an excuse to your father about why you still haven't started working on her memorial, which you insisted on handling instead of any of the amazing artists who offered to help your dad because of course they did: Everyone wants to help the great Miami.

He was already at the site, wearing one of his ridiculously large baby-blue Dolphins jerseys, even in this heat. For your whole life, everyone has called him Miami. It came from the "mi amor" your mother blurted out at the airport when she panicked and forgot his name. He was a friend of her cousin and, after her cousin was deported two months later, the only person she knew in New York. Somehow the nickname spread to your dad's friends and the other day laborers, even though you can't remember your mom saying more than five words to any of them. Your dad loved it—a big nickname for a small, timid man who was barely present in your childhood whether or not he was home.

Except that father is long gone, replaced by the warm man who is now hugging you tightly and asking about J. The transformation started gradually as his solar conversion skills became more sought after and gathered steam as he discovered his gift for teaching all the new people eagerly rushing into the sustainable construction sector. He doesn't ask you about the memorial. He just wants to know if you're okay, says you look tired. You give mostly one-word answers. You've grown to appreciate him, if not quite love him, and on most days, you're truly happy for what he's made of himself. But today you take petty pleasure in watching him struggle awkwardly in your presence. He has plenty of people celebrating who he is. Someone needs to remind him of who he was.

It was your mother's call for them to get divorced, but his passivity always forced her to make the hard decisions. This was during the wave of breakups that followed the universal income law on July 4, Women's Independence Day. But it was before the full development of the social health networks and community programs that might have prevented her from holing up in her tiny apartment now that she didn't have to go to Manhattan to clean much larger ones.

Your mom was a socialist back when your dad dismissed politics as a bunch of crap. You have a picture of her at a youth climate strike in Guatemala City. You've thought about making that the centerpiece of her memorial, but you never knew that person. You're not sure if the picture would be a celebration of her life, or an indictment of everyone who never sacrificed but still gets to live in this world she fought for but was too beaten down and isolated to truly experience.

You catch a tram from the cemetery down to work, but Douglas takes one look at your puffy face and tells you to take the day off. You try to object, but they just point up at the enormous banner hanging from the warehouse ceiling that reads "Amazon Is a Proud Lethargics Workplace."

"As you know," Doug says, "I'm a stickler for the rules." For the first time all day, you laugh. Amazonians were the first of

many subcritical unions to vote in the lethargics system, which strongly encourages people to sign up for no more than twenty hours a week and to take days off for sickness and emotional well-being. The term came from a particularly epic Jeff Bezos rant about the new world being run by "lawless lethargic losers." It's still up on his video channel, which you and your friends sometimes watch when you get high.

Doug is a good egg, really. They just get very stressed out when they're running the center. You're starting to consider voting in favor of the proposal to pay people an extra 10 percent during their managing month. Some jobs have gone that route but most Amazon sites have chosen strict pay equality, probably because of that whole Bezos "billionaire" (what a funny word!) history. In the Nile Center union meetings, most people are against manager raises, but you're hearing the vote might go differently in a few other centers like Yangtze (which handles phone repair and replacement) and Rio Grande (mending, tailoring, clothing exchange).

You thank Douglas and step outside, only to be blasted with midday heat that sends you speed-walking to the cooling center at a former mall five blocks away. The 72-degree air soothes you as you walk through the revolving door, and you head straight for the old store that has the beds where you can nap..An hour or two later you wake up energized but with a pulsing headache. You wander around the cooling center looking for something to make it go away: a soft serve cone at the ice cream station; shooting hoops in the gym; sitting in the dark mini-theatre to watch that comedy about Elon Musk's attempted coup from the moon—none of it is working.

Eventually you walk over to the medical center, where they check your vitals and offer a massage. It finally occurs to you that what you really need is someone to talk to, so you go to the food court to meet with one of the counselors on shift. As soon as you sit down, a torrent of words comes spilling out. How unfair it is that your mother was so alone, how your dad's life was no picnic but at least he had connections he could build on when the walls came down.

Now you're really letting loose. It's fine that life expectancies are slowly becoming more equal around the world, but that means nothing for the dead and mourning, so there's no equality in grief. The young white guys on the street who call out "Miami!" at your dad like he's some kind of mascot—did their wives or mothers die in their early fifties? Sure, you'll celebrate like everyone else next month on the anniversary of the surrender of the last air force drone base. But some of those celebrating lost nothing to those drones and others lost everything, and there's no committee that can do anything about that. On and on you go.

Your counselor is a sweet-looking older guy named Ray who used to be an airline mechanic at the airport where your parents met. He's been working here for a year, and really likes it, but he's no expert and can set up an appointment if you want for someone with more training. In the past year he's had more than a few conversations with people like you, especially on death anniversaries, and he's got two pieces of advice.

"First," he says, "go ahead and create a memorial for your ma based on that photo. It sounds lovely, and you know you can always change it later on."

Then he starts talking about how much he misses airplanes. He knows it's minor compared to losing a loved one, but he also lost his wife and that doesn't make him miss airplanes any less. When he worked for the airline the two of them could fly standby for free wherever they wanted, and that was what freedom meant for him back then. So when air travel was cut to reduce global emissions and most people couldn't fly anymore, he understood why it was happening, but it still left him hurt and angry for years after "the revolution."

By the way, Ray isn't the only one you know who uses those air quotes. It's how many people express the ambiguity of how exactly you all got here. Yes, there were proclamations and bombs and new governments, but those big events seemed to happen either after or before the moments when people noticed fundamental changes in their relationship to what used to be called—more air quotes—"the government."

"Second," Ray tells you, "if you want to be angry at someone for the unfairness of the past, don't torture your dad or yourself. Be pissed at me, this old white asshole who's upset we can't fly around in carbon-spewing planes anymore. Put it all on me, and I won't mind, cuz I'm getting paid to be here!"

With that he cackles, tells you he loves you and to take care of yourself, and walks away, leaving you by yourself in a food court, unsure what the hell just happened. At the next table someone is saying they heard there's still no avocado toast because the Amazon workers didn't want to come in early. You suppress a laugh and notice that your headache is fading.

Tomorrow you'll go in early, show Douglas some love, give the people their avocados, call your dad. Today you're going to go ahead and get that massage, have another ice cream cone, and then go home to tell J about your plans for the memorial. And if it's still this freaking hot out tonight, you're turning on the damn emergency AC.

10.

WILL SOCIALISM BE BORING?

The year was 2081, and everybody was finally equal. They weren't only equal before God and the law. They were equal every which way. Nobody was smarter than anybody else. Nobody was better looking than anybody else. Nobody was stronger or quicker than anybody else. All this equality was due to the 211th, 212th, and 213th Amendments to the Constitution, and to the unceasing vigilance of agents of the United States Handicapper General.

That's the opening to Kurt Vonnegut's "Harrison Bergeron," a short story about a future society with the most strictly enforced equality. Attractive people are forced to wear masks, smart people have earpieces that regularly distract their thoughts with loud noises, and so on. As one would expect with Vonnegut, there are some darkly hilarious moments—such as a ballet performance in which the dancers are shackled with leg weights—but unlike most of his stories, "Harrison Bergeron" is based on a reactionary premise: equality can only be achieved by reducing the most talented down to the mediocre ranks of the masses.

Socialism has frequently been portrayed in popular science fiction in these types of gray dystopian terms, which reflects the conflicted relationship that many artists have with capitalism. People who make a living through their creativity are often repulsed by the anti-human values and commercialized culture of their society but are also aware of their unique status within it that allows them to express their individuality—as long as it sells. They fear that socialism would strip them of that status and reduce them to the level of mere workers—because even those whose job is to dream up time travel and alternate dimensions sometimes can't imagine a world that values and encourages the artistic expression of all of its members.*

There's another reason that socialist societies are imagined to be grim and dreary: societies that have called themselves socialist have often been kind of grim and dreary. Shortly after the revolutions in Eastern Europe that ended the domination of the Soviet Union, the Rolling Stones played a legendary concert in Prague in which they were welcomed as cultural heroes.† The catch is that this was 1990, Mick and Keith were almost fifty, and it had been years since their most recent hit, a song called "Harlem Shuffle" that is god-awful. Forget about the censored books and the bans on demonstrations. If you want to understand how stifling Stalinist societies were, watch the video for "Harlem Shuffle" and then think about one of the coolest cities in Europe going out of its mind with joy at the chance to see those guys.‡

Does it really matter if socialism is boring? Perhaps it seems silly, even offensive, to be concerned about such a trivial matter at a time when the world is being battered by rising sea levels and fascist hate. We may enjoy movies about thrilling struggles to save the universe, but most of us prefer a reality of predictability and routine. That's how we ended up with President Joe Biden, whose unspoken campaign slogan against both Bernie Sanders and Donald Trump was "Make America Boring Again."

Worrying that socialism might be boring can seem like the ultimate expression of privilege: *Sure, it would be nice to eliminate poverty,*

---

* This is not true about all successful science fiction writers, as outraged fans of Octavia E. Butler, Ursula Le Guin, and Kim Stanley Robinson will probably remind me.

† The Stones concert is the setting for Tom Stoppard's *Rock 'n' Roll*, an insightful play about those who rejected Stalinism and those who stuck with it until the bitter end.

‡ Okay, it's not as bad as the prison labor camps, repressing revolutions in Hungary, Czechoslovakia, and Poland, and ruining the name of communism, but that song is appalling.

war, and racism . . . but what if I get bored? But it does matter because we don't want to live in a society without creativity and excitement, and also because if those things are being stifled then there must be a certain ruling clique or class that is doing the stifling—whether or not they think it's for our own good. Finally, if socialism is stale and static, it will never be able to replace capitalism, which can accurately be called many nasty things, but boring is not one of them.

Capitalism has revolutionized the world many times over in the past two hundred years and changed how we think, look, communicate, and work. In the past few decades, this system adapted quickly and effectively to the global wave of protests and strikes in the sixties and seventies. Unionized factories were closed and relocated to other corners of the world, the stated role of government was shifted from helping people to helping corporations help people, and finally all these changes and others as well were sold to us as what the protesters had been fighting for all along—a world in which every man, woman, and child is born with the equal right to buy as many smartphones and factory-ripped pairs of jeans as they want. When people then used those smartphones to assemble against this new era of global inequality in the Arab Spring and Occupy, the system adapted again, promoting Twitter and Facebook (and capitalism itself) as revolutionary "disrupters" even as the real disrupters were being arrested and tortured.

Capitalism can reinvent itself far more quickly than any previous economic order. In *The Communist Manifesto* Marx and Engels write that while earlier class societies desperately tried to maintain the status quo, capitalism thrives on overturning it:

> Conservation of the old modes of production in unaltered form, was . . . the first condition of existence for all earlier industrial classes. Constant revolutionising of production, uninterrupted disturbance of all social conditions, everlasting uncertainty and agitation distinguish the [capitalist] epoch from all earlier ones.

The result is a world in constant motion. Yesterday's factory district is today's slum is tomorrow's hipster neighborhood. "All that is solid melts into air." That's another line from the *Manifesto* and also the name of a wonderful book by Marshall Berman, who writes that to live in modern capitalism is "to find ourselves in an environment that promises us adventure, power, joy, growth, transformation of ourselves and the world—and at the same time, that threatens to destroy everything we have, everything we know, everything we are."

Yet most of our lives are far from exciting. We work for bosses who want us to be mindless drones. Even when a cool new invention comes to our workplace, we can count on it to eventually be used to make us do more work in less time, which might arouse the passions of management but will only fill our days with more drudgery. Outside of work, it's the same story. Schools see their primary role as providing "career readiness," a nice way to describe getting kids accustomed to the demeaning depression of work.

Even the few hours that are supposed to be our own are mostly spent on laundry, cooking, cleaning, checking homework, and all the other necessary tasks to get ourselves and our families ready for work the next day. I was just poking fun at the cultural boredom of twentieth-century Eastern Europe, but there's compelling evidence that, as flawed as state socialism was, its guarantees of housing, income, and child care allowed people—especially women—to have happier marriages and better sex.*

Most of us only experience the excitement of capitalism as something happening somewhere else: new gadgets for rich people, wild parties for celebrities, fun dances by teenagers in mansions that we watch on our phones while scarfing down dinner. (On the bright side, at least most of it is better than "Harlem Shuffle.") Even worse, when we do get to directly touch the excitement, it's usually because we're on the business end of it. It's our jobs being replaced by that incredible new robot, our rent becoming too expensive ever since the beautiful luxury tower was built across the street.

---

* Oh, what a surprise. After ignoring a bunch of my footnotes, *now* you're all down here. Whatever. Check out Kristen Ghodsee's *Why Women Have Better Sex Under Socialism* for an interesting look at women's lives under Eastern European state socialism, not just in terms of sex but also . . . and you've already left to find the other book. *Sigh.*

Adding insult to injury, we are then told if we complain that we are standing in the way of progress. The sacrifice of individuals in the name of societal progress is said to be one of the horrors of socialism, a world run by faceless bureaucrats supposedly acting for the common good. But there are plenty of invisible and unelected decision makers under capitalism: search engine algorithm designers who decide what we see online; health insurance managers who decide from a cubicle whether our surgery is "unnecessary"; FBI field agents who decide what list to put us on based on a protest or mosque we attend.

Socialism also involves plenty of change, upheaval, and even chaos. But this chaos comes, as Hal Draper might have said, from below. One month after the October Revolution, the Bolshevik-led soviet government removed marriage from the control of the church and allowed couples to get divorced at the request of either partner. These laws dramatically changed family dynamics and women's lives, as evidenced by some of the song lyrics that became popular in rural Russian villages:

> *Time was when my husband used his fists and force.*
> *But now he is so tender. For he fears divorce.*
> *I no longer fear my husband.*
> *If we can't cooperate,*
> *I will take myself to court,*
> *and we will separate.**

Of course, divorce can be heartbreaking as well as liberating. Revolutions cast everything in a new light, from our leaders to our loved ones. Trotsky movingly described this process in a 1923 article for the Soviet newspaper *Pravda*:

> Gigantic events have descended on the family in its old shape, the war and the revolution. And following them came creeping slowly the underground mole—critical thought, the conscious study and evaluation of family relations and forms of life. No wonder that

* For these and other great tidbits of sex and love in revolutionary Russia, listen to Jason Yanowitz's talk "Sex and Sexuality in Soviet Russia" at WeAreMany.org.

> this process reacts in the most intimate and hence most painful way on family relationships.

In another article, Trotsky described daily experience in revolutionary Russia as "the process by which everyday life for the working masses is being broken up and formed anew." In the same way that today we experience capitalist processes of gentrification and automation, these first steps toward socialism offered both the promise of creation and the threat of destruction.

But the crucial difference is that the people Trotsky wrote about were playing an active role in determining how their world was changing. They were far from having complete control, especially over the mass poverty and illiteracy that the tsar and world war had bequeathed to them. But even in these miserable conditions, the years between the October Revolution and Stalin's final consolidation of power demonstrated the excitement of a society in which new doors were open to the majority classes for the first time.

There was an explosion of art and culture. Cutting-edge painters and sculptors decorated the public squares of Russian cities with their futurist art. Lenin hated the futurists, but this didn't stop the government from funding their journal *Art of the Commune*. Ballets and theaters were opened up to mass audiences. Cultural groups and workers' committees came together to bring art and artistic training into factories. The filmmaker Sergei Eisenstein gained world renown for the groundbreaking technique of his movies depicting the Russian Revolution. Unlike the silly premise of "Harrison Bergeron," socialism didn't find talented artists to be a threat to "equality." There was no conflict between appreciating individual artists and opening up the previously exclusive art world to the masses of workers and peasants.

The possibilities of socialism that the world glimpsed in Russia for a few years was not a sterile experiment controlled by a handful of theorists. It was a messy and thrilling creation of tens of millions of people, groping toward a different way of running society and treating one another with all the skills, impediments, and neuroses they had acquired through living under capitalism, and in the horrible circumstances of a poor war-torn country. They screwed up in all sorts of ways, but they also showed that socialism is a real possibility, not an immaculate illusion that can't meet the passionate needs of real human beings. And the society they were pointing toward was one where equality meant not lowering but raising the overall cultural and intellectual level of society. In many novels, movies, and other artistic renderings of socialism, there is little mention of rising divorce rates or heated debates about art. Most of them imagine societies without conflict, which is why they seem so creepy.*

A related problem happens inside many protest movements and socialist organizations, which can be unprepared to handle internal disagreements among people who are all on the same side. Differences of opinion on the left can too often be treated as betrayals of trust, friendship, or principle. Some groups try to avoid this problem through a consensus model, which means that almost everybody present has to agree on a decision for it to get passed. Consensus can be an effective way to foster collaboration among people who don't know and trust one another, especially because most people in this supposedly democratic society have almost no experience participating in the democratic process of discussion, debate, and then a majority-rule vote.†

When we view consensus not only as a temporary tactic but as a model for how society should be run, however, there is a problem. I want to live in a democratic society with conflicts and arguments, where people aren't afraid to stand up for what they believe in and don't feel pressured to soften their opinions so that, when a compromise is reached, we can pretend that we all agreed in the first place. If your case for socialism rests on the idea that people will stop getting

---

* A wonderful exception is Ursula K. Le Guin's *The Dispossessed*, which is set on a planet with a truly anarchist society that is both succeeding in creating a vibrant classless society and struggling with issues like conformity and bureaucratization.

† In *The Take*, a documentary by Naomi Klein and Avi Lewis about factory occupations in Argentina in the 2000s, there's a wonderful moment when a worker explains that at first people would get angry after they lost a vote in the factory committee, but that over time "we got used to winning and we got used to losing."

into arguments and even occasionally acting like jerks, you should probably find another cause.

"We can (and must) begin to build socialism," Lenin once wrote, "not with abstract human material, or with human material specially prepared by us, but with the human material bequeathed to us by capitalism. True, that is no easy matter, but no other approach to this task is serious enough to warrant discussion."

To be an effective socialist, it is extremely helpful to like human beings. Not "humanity" but real, sweaty people. In *All That Is Solid Melts into Air*, Berman tells a story about Robert Moses, the famous New York City public planner who flattened entire neighborhoods that stood in the way of the exact spots where he envisioned new highways. Moses, a friend once said, "loved the public, but not as people." He built parks, beaches, and highways for the masses to use, even as he loathed most of the working-class New Yorkers he encountered.

Loving the public but not people has also been a feature of elitist socialists, whose faith lay more in five-year development plans, utopian blueprints, or campaign platforms than on the wonders that hundreds of millions can achieve when they are inspired and liberated. That is why their visions for socialism could be lifeless and unimaginative. By contrast, Marx, who is generally portrayed as an isolated intellectual, was a rowdy, argumentative, funny, passionate person who once declared that his favorite saying was the maxim: "I am a human being, I consider nothing that is human alien to me."

I find it hard to see how a world run by the majority of human beings, with all of our gloriously and infuriatingly varied talents, personalities, madnesses, and passions, could possibly be boring.

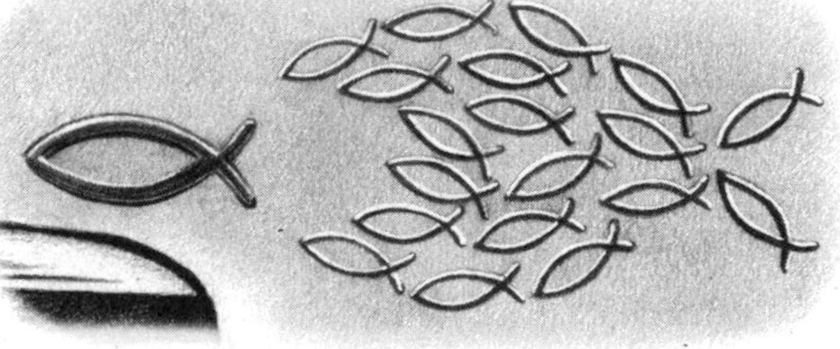

11.

THE GOOD NEWS

Socialists have an unwarranted reputation for being against any and all forms of religion. To be fair, it's easy to take some of the things we say out of context. For example, you might hear a socialist criticize *bourgeois morality* and conclude that she thinks the very concept of morality is somehow *bourgeois,* which is nonsense and makes her sound like a posh villain sitting in a high-back chair stroking a long-haired cat. What the comrade is actually referring to is the version of morality we have under capitalism, where stealing a little makes you a criminal and stealing a lot makes you a CEO.

Then there's one of Karl Marx's best-known quotes: "Religion is the opium of the people." Taken out of context, as the line usually is, it sounds condescending. But read the entire passage it comes from, and the meaning changes entirely:

> Religious suffering is, at one and the same time, the expression of real suffering and a protest against real suffering. Religion is the sigh of the oppressed creature, the heart of a heartless world, and the soul of soulless conditions. It is the opium of the people.
>
> The abolition of religion as the illusory happiness of the people is the demand for their real happiness. To call on them to give up their illusions about their condition is to call on them to give up a condition that requires illusions.

Marx was less concerned about whether people believed in heaven than about a world that drives many to hope they'll be happier when they're dead. There are many socialists who don't believe in God, but we should have nothing to do with those atheists who mock spiritual beliefs or claim that religion is the root of all our problems—especially if they have nothing to say about the "soulless conditions" of capitalism. I have particular contempt for those who use religious skepticism as a cover for demonizing Islam. These supposed liberal freethinkers are really just lazy racists who want to wage a modern-day Crusade without having to get up in the morning for church.

If religion is defined as a way that we try to understand what place our tiny insignificant lives have in the giant scary universe, then socialists don't oppose religion any more than we could entirely reject culture, philosophy, or other foundations of the human intellect. We don't agree with many of the explanations that organized religions put forward to explain the world, and we often find ourselves opposed to their powerful and wealthy leaders. But you could say the same thing for university administrations and Hollywood studios, and it doesn't mean that socialists are against college and movies.*

It's especially critical for socialists to connect with religious beliefs at a time when the world is beset with disasters of fire and flood that seem to come straight out of the Bible. A 2015 YouGov poll found that Americans fear the apocalypse in similar numbers regardless of political affiliation, but that Democrats are more likely to see the cause as climate change, while Republicans cite Judgment Day. It's a sign of how successfully we are divided by the stupidity of two-party culture war that few of us can recognize them as the same thing. Of course, there are scientific explanations for the effects of rising levels of carbon in the atmosphere, but physics is just another way of understanding that we live in violation of laws that are bigger than humankind. Whether or not you share Daniel Wildcat's belief

* When I first joined a socialist group in the 1990s, a friend asked if I was "still allowed to watch TV" as if I had moved into a monastery. In fact, my list of approved programs was almost two pages long! I even won the right to watch *The Fresh Prince of Bel-Air* once I assured the party leaders that it wasn't pro-monarchy. (The setup to that joke is a true story, by the way. You have no idea what it was like being a socialist before Bernie.)

that the climate crisis is "Mother Earth . . . trying to tell us something," it's clear that capitalism is reaping what it has sown.

My point is not that socialists should seek "common ground" with any bigot who can quote scripture. It's that we should celebrate the socialist ideas that exist inside every religion and acknowledge the aspects of socialism that are at least somewhat faith-based and even spiritual. Then we can expose some of the cynical frauds who call themselves "faith leaders."

Church and State

Politics, not religion, is the reason why fundamentalist Christians have been organized to persecute trans children rather than forming a militant bloc of holy warriors against the destructive greed of Big Oil. For much of US history, evangelicals were at the heart of radical movements for change—from the anti-slavery abolitionists to the populist poor farmers. But starting in the 1970s, leaders of the new "Christian right" entered a pact with business conservatives, supporting corporate tax breaks and anti-labor laws in return for all-out attacks on abortion and LGBTQ people. This unholy alliance became laughable but remained effective when the pastors went all in for Donald Trump, the godless freak and Jeffrey Epstein wingman that even atheists can't believe hasn't been struck down by lightning.

As a result, it's rare to hear fiery sermons from pulpits about how global burning is a divine signal that humanity should repent from our planet-destroying ways. Instead, many devout Christians find themselves inside the Fox News echo chamber of climate denial, with preachers who think gender neutral pronouns will bring the end of the world but dismiss the actual hellfire that arrives each summer as a socialist hoax cooked up by George Soros and the Chinese government.

I am obviously disturbed by the conspiracy theories of climate denialists, but I almost sympathize with their plight. It must suck to be a conservative at a time when the only realistic ways of dealing with climate change—prioritizing health and lives over energy companies, long-term planning over short-term profits, and international cooperation over nationalist competition—sound an awful lot like socialism. Putting myself in their shoes, I try to imagine climate researchers declaring that rising temperatures can only be stopped by building a wall on the US-Mexico border—made up entirely of Confederate statues: I wouldn't believe such "science," and neither would you. Okay, that was a really dumb scenario, but I'm trying to express just how intolerable actual science has become for those dedicated to the capitalist status quo.

If climate change already made it seem as if the universe had a secret socialist agenda, when COVID hit there was a moment when it seemed like we were actually living inside an extremely didactic communist play from the 1930s:

> *Worker #1: Brothers and sisters, to survive this virus we'll have to put human lives above economic interests!*
>
> *Worker #2: That's right, comrade. Everyone, stay home from work until the danger has passed! Empty out the crowded prisons and detention centers!*
>
> *Worker #1: Don't forget that we must share vaccines with everyone around the world or else the virus might develop new variants and kill us all! None of us are safe until all of us are safe!**

Conservative religious leaders are leaving a moral and spiritual vacuum when it comes to humanity's existential threat, and socialists shouldn't be shy about helping to fill it. Now more than ever, socialism can be credibly seen as not just a more democratic and humane society but also as a way of life that's more in tune with whatever

---

* None of this happened, of course. Instead, after a brief period of shutdown and shock, business went back to normal, jails stayed full, vaccines weren't shared, immune-compromised folks didn't matter, and we acted like it was totally normal for thousands of people to die daily and millions more to have long-term illness. This was generally referred to as "the *new* reality," a low-key acknowledgment that there had once been a different reality—one where COVID was bad and should be avoided—but it was annoying so we had it replaced.

Larger Plan you subscribe to, be it God, Nature, or the well-being of future generations. So when Republicans scream that the Green New Deal and other climate change measures are part of a communist conspiracy, let's not deny it. Instead, we can concede that our proposals to preserve life on Earth do in fact look a lot like radical democracy and wealth redistribution, but (and maybe we can pause here and shrug as we cast a shy glance skyward) who are we to question the will of the Creator?

Capitalism has always had a problem fulfilling our spiritual needs because it can't allow anything to get in the way of the profit imperative. As the *Communist Manifesto* memorably put it:

> All fixed, fast-frozen relations, with their train of ancient and venerable prejudices and opinions, are swept away, all new-formed ones become antiquated before they can ossify. All that is solid melts into air, all that is holy is profaned, and man is at last compelled to face with sober senses his real conditions of life, and his relations with his kind.

But over time, every dominant order has tried to find a higher meaning in its rule, and capitalism is no exception. That's why economic theories we're taught in school borrow heavily from religion in a way that would have baffled Adam Smith. God is now cast as Free Market, an invisible but omnipresent force that sometimes works in mysterious ways but should never be questioned because we live according to Its law. When economies succeed, all praise is due to Free Market. When they fail, we must have done something to anger It, like raising the minimum wage or limiting how much factories can pollute the air. We mortals cannot possibly grasp the complexities of the millions of economic relationships that we ourselves have created. To interfere with Free Market in an attempt to plan and direct the economy is to commit the cardinal sin of pride, and meet a fate similar to the boy who flew too close to the sun.* Belgian socialist

* Yes, I know I'm confusing Christianity with Greek mythology. My religious foundation was a year of bar mitzvah lessons, *Jesus Christ Superstar*, and the Percy Jackson books. You didn't pick up this book for the theology.

Ernest Mandel writes that the mythology surrounding the unknowable workings of the market suggests that "humanity's insight into the laws of its own evolution [is] a fruit from which it should be forbidden to partake."

Capitalism has answers to existential questions that all religions aim to address:

What is my place in the universe?

To compete in the rat race, and surrender my fate to the Invisible Hand.

What is the meaning of life?

To have more tomorrow than I have today.*

These are the sacred tenets across the world today. Christian presidents and Hindu prime ministers are equally committed to the dogma of capital's everlasting growth. But capitalist ideology isn't enriching enough to be a religion. It doesn't tell us if we have a soul, or help us to understand what happens after we die. It doesn't have a deity for us to worship, although it produces more than a few billionaires who think otherwise. Anyone with more spiritual depth than your average Wall Street sociopath won't find satisfaction in these narrow goals. This is one reason why the older religions are still very much in force, guiding dietary habits, community bonds, and voting patterns for billions of people.

But while capitalism is happy to take advantage of religious traditions that have stood the test of millennia, its primary spiritual partner is nationalism. In *Imagined Communities*, the political scientist Benedict Anderson argues that nationalism has in recent centuries taken up many of the roles that religion used to play. The title of his book describes the primary one: nationalism makes us feel connected with millions of people we'll never meet but who live inside the same invisible borders. It also spiritually ties us to past generations we call our founding fathers, even if our own ancestors lived halfway around the world.

---

* Most people aren't selfish enough to believe this, so we accept the related precept that life is about our children having more than we do, which sounds more generous but in practice means pretty much the same thing, only with more streaming fees.

Nationalism balances out capitalism's extreme individualism by giving us something to belong to and sacrifice for: "A country is more than an economy," as a recent presidential advisor put it. But just as with capitalism, there are nasty terms and conditions hidden beneath the noble-sounding ideals. That seemingly harmless quote came from Trump guru Steve Bannon when he argued that Asians were taking too many tech jobs and that foreign college students should be kicked out of the US after they graduate. Just as the state provides all the necessary services and support that bosses are too focused on short-term profit to handle, nationalism is there to fill in the many holes of purpose and meaning that capitalism leaves empty. And in times of crisis when capitalism leaves even more holes than usual, the appeal of nationalism can grow, along with the threat of fascism.

Liberals oppose right-wing nationalism (usually), and can be important allies against the far right. But just as liberals look to improve instead of replace capitalism, they try to counter bad nationalism with their own happy version. "Now look here," they'll say to Steve Bannon. "Racism is un-American!" This is about as effective as saying "bad kitty!" when presented with another dead mouse on your doorstep. Cats are killing machines, and America is a racism machine. Claiming otherwise might be well-intentioned and aspirational, but it's also delusional gaslighting that implies that people outside the US are more racist, which is . . . well . . . racist.

Is Socialism a Religion?

Like religion, nationalism isn't an idea that can be proven wrong in debate. It's a means of finding fellowship and meaning, which can only be replaced by building alternative forms of community, real and imagined. There have been times in history when socialist organizations have been able to do just that for millions of working people—only for liberals and conservatives alike to dismiss them as fanatics. This is one of the headaches socialists face: we're denounced by some as godless heathens even as others accuse us of being hucksters trying to build a new church promising workers their very own kingdom of heaven.

One of the most famous instances of this second critique came in the title of the book *The God That Failed,* which was written by disillusioned former Communist Party supporters after they and the rest of the world discovered Stalin's crimes in Russia. Given the historic betrayals covered in the book, I don't mind the choice of title—except I'm not sure why socialism would be singled out for failure by anyone writing in the late 1940s. In the wake of the Nazi Holocaust and the nuclear devastation of Hiroshima and Nagasaki, what grade did the authors think regular God deserved: a C+?

Socialism is no god, but there have been many who integrate it into their religious belief—especially in Latin American churches influenced by liberation theology. But even the most secular socialist parties have been shaped by religious traditions. Karl Kautsky, the most influential Marxist in the generation after Marx, wrote extensively about Christianity's origins as a doctrine of the oppressed inside the Roman Empire. "Socialism," he once declared, "is no message of woe for the proletariat but rather good news, a new gospel." Many European socialist parties—including the Bolsheviks—took Kautsky's message to heart, confidently spreading their updated version of the Bible's "good news": the working class's historic destiny to overthrow capitalism and create a better world.*

Another reason why socialism has been accused of sneaking religious fervor into secular politics is the whole "socialism or barbarism" thing. Long before Rosa Luxemburg made her famous ultimatum at the outset of World War I, Marx and Engels wrote that there were times in history when the way a society has been economically organized becomes a barrier to its further development, a crisis that can produce a revolutionary new society or a disastrous "common ruin of the contending classes." They were thinking of the Roman Empire's inability to move beyond its reliance on conquest and slavery, which led to its collapse into the Western European Dark Ages. Still, it isn't hard to see how this framework builds on longstanding ideas of heaven and hell, as well as the Church's role in elevating people's

---

* This comes from Lars Lih, a leading historian of the European socialist movement in the early twentieth century.

ordinary daily struggles into an epic clash with the fate of the world hanging in the balance.

Some of these prophetic themes haven't aged so well after a century of failed revolutions and betrayed hopes with no socialist paradise in sight. It's fair to say that our predecessors might have a bit of tunnel vision. We can see more clearly now that Marx and others had a tendency at times to make the collapse of capitalism seem inevitable and to underestimate the system's ability to resolve its deep crises (at the terrible expense of poor people and the planet) and evolve into different forms—including some that went by the name of socialism.

But that doesn't mean that it's wrong to build movements imbued with faith and a sense of destiny. Marx's key contribution was his analysis of how socialism is not just morally correct but in the material self-interest of all those who produce the world's wealth. But while self-interest is a powerful motivator, so is people's desire for lives that are meaningful and in accordance with a higher truth. For socialism to become strong enough to shut down oil pipelines and turn soldiers against their generals, it needs to reach people on both of these levels. And it can.

Socialism offers an alternative to capitalism that is richer in every sense of the word. We make the bold but reasonable claim that humanity is capable of taking control of the markets and structures we have created, and using them to elevate cooperation over competition. This allows socialism to overcome capitalism's moral failure of relentless individualism. Socialism doesn't disregard our individuality. It adds to it while making it part of something bigger. Marx and Engels wrote in the *Manifesto* that under socialism "the free development of each becomes the condition for the free development of all." Terry Eagleton elaborates:

> In this sense, socialism does not simply reject [capitalist] liberal society, with its passionate commitment to the individual. Instead, it builds on and completes it. In doing so, it shows how some of the contradictions of liberalism, in which your freedom may flourish only at the expense of mine, may be resolved. Only through others

> can we finally come into our own. This means an enrichment of individual freedom, not a diminishing of it. It is hard to think of a finer ethics. On a personal level, it is known as love.

I wouldn't recommend that socialists start a new organized religion unless I get to be High Priest.* But a socialist society could offer healthier answers to some of the Big Questions:

What is my place in the universe?

To develop my individual abilities and work with others to best restore, enhance, and enjoy this miraculous world that's been entrusted to our care.

What is the meaning of . . . Yeah, I'm not going to go there.

Just as socialism has more satisfying spiritual answers than capitalism, so can internationalism create a more fulfilling community than nationalism. There's a very different sense of belonging that can take place when millions of non-imagined people come together across borders. I've experienced this feeling on three occasions to date. The international day of protest against the US war in Iraq in February 2003 and the Women's Marches that greeted Trump's 2016 inauguration around the world were both days where angry demonstrations turned into joyous celebrations of ordinary people as a planetary force for peace and love. Some might read that last sentence with a cynical smirk because neither protest "won." I wish them the chance to experience such a moment themselves someday soon and judge for themselves.†

As powerful as those days were, the experience of 2011 was something else entirely, taking place across a full year. Dictators were toppled and shaken in the Arab Spring, public squares were taken over

---

* Dibs!

† While the antiwar movement and Women's Marches had their limitations, both had real impacts. The first laid the groundwork for public opinion turning against the Iraq War within a few years. The second put the Trump administration on the defensive by making it clear that he didn't have majority support. Both also forced Democrats to act at least somewhat like an opposition party—until the protests stopped and they could get back to fundraising.

in Spain and Greece, and the Occupy movement spread from Wall Street to cities across the world. As people rose up, they discovered one another and themselves. Teachers, construction workers, veterans, and immigrants came together in Cairo's Tahrir Square, the Wisconsin Capitol building, and urban plazas across Greece and Spain. Occupying public space was a demand for democracy and equality but also a practical way for working-class people to see one another and understand just how powerful they could be. New lines of communication were established not just within societies but also between them, the beginning of a worldwide conversation among ordinary people. The international ruling class has regular summits and conferences to discuss how the world should be run. 2011 provided a glimpse of how the international working class could do the same—partly through social media platforms problematically owned by our enemies but even more through the language of mass action.

The global dialogue was kicked off by Tunisians declaring that it was time to rise up against US-backed dictatorships. Egyptians responded by occupying Tahrir Square in Cairo, which spread the message to millions in Libya, Yemen, Bahrain, and Syria. Elsewhere, working people occupied the Wisconsin capitol building and public plazas across Spain and Greece, broadcasting that it was time for people beyond the Middle East to rise up. Within months, a few hundred activists in New York City took the conversation to the fortress of the worldwide enemy, branded the movement Occupy Wall Street, and gave the conversation a common vocabulary of the One Percent and the Ninety-Nine Percent. Eventually, dialogue was forcefully cut off, but tens of millions briefly experienced a sense of belonging to something entirely different than nation, race, or religion.

I Believe That We Can Win

The bigger danger for radicals today is not false certainty that the revolution is on its way but rather despair that it will never come. The crises of our world have turned us to socialism in historic numbers but also switched our brains into the emergency self-preservation mode better known as anxiety. Our frightened isolation—eagerly exploited by social media companies searching our phones for more information to sell—is a problem that is both personal and political. For socialism to win support that's both wide and deep, it's got to embody not just a slogan but a community, not just policies but a social trust that there are many millions out there who will have our backs and "fight for someone we don't know."

That's the wonderful pledge Bernie Sanders asked his supporters to make during his 2020 presidential campaign. It's as good a slogan as any for the socialist world we want to win, but it's also not a world most have ever lived in. Few people belong to unions, tenant organizations, or neighborhood organizations, and even fewer have succeeded in working with others to win a raise, stop a deportation, or challenge sexual harassment. Instead, our life experiences have trained us not to trust our hopes that things can get better and pay close attention to our fears that they can get even worse.

It's easy to forget—because we are encouraged to—that we aren't always alone. When people took to the streets in desperation during COVID lockdowns because they couldn't take another police murder of an unarmed Black person, they discovered, to their desperate relief, hundreds of thousands and then tens of millions doing the same: we weren't alone. When they rushed to the nearest airport in January 2017 to demand that Muslim passengers be allowed in the country in defiance of Trump's travel ban, we weren't alone. When four thousand veterans traveled to the freezing encampment at Standing Rock a few months earlier to form a human shield around water protectors and apologize for the US military's crimes against Native Americans, most of us were watching by ourselves from our little screens, but we weren't alone.

Once these movements end, as movements usually do, some proclaim that we shouldn't have fallen for their promises. And because we are alone again, we listen to these voices more than we should. But do we really think the spirit of Tahrir Square and Standing Rock are gone just because we can't see them? Ideas have been planted across the globe, and we're going to need millions of socialists to feed those seeds with hope, protect their shoots with belief, and make them organizationally and intellectually powerful enough to weather all the poison this world can pour on them.

We protect those seeds with protests and campaigns, with study groups and mutual aid. We nurture them by coming together for rituals, stories, and maybe some drinking on May Day, International Women's Day, Juneteenth, Pride, and Indigenous People's Day. We build and make donations to organizations that can spread our collective message and develop our individual potential. We try to build a loving, restorative heart in a heartless world without losing focus on how to get to a different one, not in the next life but in the coming years.

I was raised as a secular Jew and that's what I remain. I don't think of our tasks in terms of *mitzvahs, crusades, jihads,* or *repairing our relations with Mother Earth,* but you can and should if it suits you. Religious phrasing definitely has more popular appeal than Marx's not-so-spicy "at a certain stage of development, the material productive forces of society come into conflict with the existing relations of production." The facts are that oceans are rising, disease stalks the land, the oppressed are rising up, and there are wicked people among us. At a certain point the fool is not she who sees the connections between everything but she who cannot.

While I'm an atheist, I would never call myself a nonbeliever. I believe in higher powers inside people that can only be activated in a society designed to bring them out. My belief in these powers is so strong that I have organized my life around them, despite the fact that I cannot prove their existence. Of course, I have doubts—all believers do—and some days they overwhelm me. So the next day I try to take strength from those around me who are standing strong, and I hope this book can do the same for some of you. Religions need congregations, and socialists need organizations to help us support one another and keep us accountable and disciplined to stay on the path of hope over fear.

It takes a certain degree of faith to devote yourself to a cause you can't always see—not a dogma to hide behind in the face of challenging new ideas and circumstances, but a confidence to keep fighting for your vision of a different world. We don't know exactly what that world will look like, or how long it will take to win it, because those answers aren't in any bibles, religious or secular. We're going to have to write that history ourselves.

Can I get an *amen*?

ODDLY SPECIFIC ADVICE ON WHAT TO DO NEXT

Gently close the back cover over the final page. Close your eyes and release a soft whistle of appreciation for the wit and wisdom you have just received. Extend that feeling of gratitude to all the wonderful people in your life for whom you can buy this book as a present. But that is for later. Now it's time to plan your next step. You're going to want to run out right away and find the first socialist gathering you can—but wait. You should probably eat something in case they don't put out snacks. Take out a jar of peanut butter . . .

Sorry, but I can't give exact instructions on how to put these ideas into practice. For one thing, unlike Google and the National Security Agency, I don't know who or where you are.

You could be a high school student in 2025, a warehouse worker helping to lead (knock on wood) the great global Amazon Strike of 2026, or a politically conscious power forward who has just led the Knicks to the 2047 NBA championship. Okay, that last one is never going to happen, but my point is that this book is intended to provide people in a wide range of circumstances with the introductory socialist ideas to help them figure out what kind of organizations, campaigns, and strategies they want to pursue.

There's another reason why I can't tell you exactly what to do next: I don't quite know myself. I've been writing this book during a world-changing pandemic whose long-term consequences are still largely unknown. COVID has broken society's already fragile bonds of trust in common sources of information and truth, but it has also shaken the until-then-unquestioned assumption that it's natural to spend most of our lives at work. It has frayed supply lines and psyches, and shown that even the US is not immune to plagues and other forces of history. The coming years could see elections degenerate into street fighting or street protests escalate into general strikes. Perhaps neither scenario is likely, but not as unlikely as the return to a "normal" that many people long for even as they are starting to forget exactly what it looked like.

Back in 2014, the . . . *Seriously* in this book's title was a self-deprecating joke about how marginalized these ideas were from mainstream society. In less than a decade, socialism has come back to prominence but, more spectacularly, capitalism has revealed itself to be the flaming bag of dog poop that it's always been but had at least been able to cover up most of the time. Now the name of the book reads differently. . . . *Seriously* is more demand than joke. I thought maybe I should change it to *Socialism . . . Desperately.**

This worldwide period of uncertainty has coincided with a personal one. The year before COVID saw the dissolution of the socialist group I was a member of for my entire adult life. The International Socialist Organization was a small group that did meaningful work over four difficult decades. But it was unable to adapt to socialism's return to the mainstream, and the resulting fractures revealed a deeply flawed and at times abusive internal culture. The group's dissolution was a hard, humbling, and necessary process that pushed me (and many others) to belatedly explore more of the wonderful radical thinkers outside my own tradition, a process that I've tried to incorporate into this second edition of the book.

The experiences of the last few years, both for the world and my own little corner of it, didn't shake my certainty that socialism will win, because I never had that. What has changed is my determination to be as honest as possible about my uncertainties about the path ahead, without wavering in my conviction (which remains firm) that a democratic and revolutionary socialism is both possible and necessary. In that exasperatingly vague spirit, I offer a few pieces of wisdom that I've picked up over the years:

---

* My cousin proposed *Socialism . . . See, I Fucking Told You!*

Get organized, again and again.

You can't be much of a socialist without being part of an organization. Ideas are only as good as the organized forces that can make them a reality—and those ideas are usually better when they come from people who are part of groups that facilitate debate and discussion among members with various talents, experiences, and insights.

Not long ago, most activists were unaffiliated free agents, organizing through social media and temporary coalitions, which worked well around specific issues but didn't do much to build and train the forces we need to take on capitalism in the long run. Now it's become a commonsense idea on the left that you accomplish more as part of an organization than as an individual. This is a great development. Just remember that organizations are tools for achieving our collective goals. These tools need to be cared for, maintained, and sharpened. But at some point they also break down, and then it's time to build or find new ones.

Don't be a snob.

Becoming a socialist is an eye-opening experience. You start noticing so many aspects of the world that are unfair or just silly that you had never questioned before. Each observation makes the case for socialism that much more obvious to you, to the point that you don't understand why your coworkers and friends don't see it. This is an old problem on the left. Many wide-eyed students who went to their first anti–Vietnam War protest in 1967 thinking that the war was an honest mistake on the part of the president had by 1968 become jaded radicals who looked down on noobs for being so naïve as to think the war was an honest mistake on the part of the president. Don't be that guy. Not only is it obnoxious, it's the worst way to build support for our side.

Learn the Serenity Prayer.

At every meeting of Alcoholics Anonymous, people recite the following words: "God grant me the serenity to accept the things I cannot change, courage to change the things I can, and wisdom to know the difference." This is not a bad approach to the task of being a socialist, whether or not capitalism has driven you to excessive drinking. We need the boldness to stand up for our ideas in the face of a hostile capitalist society and also the patience to understand that it is not we alone but the larger working class that has the power to make those ideas a reality. We have to recognize the factors that we can currently control in order to make our numbers as large as possible in preparation for those rare historical moments we can't control when hundreds of millions of people decide to resist.

On a related note, the only way we can get this balance somewhat right is to freely debate with one another about the best way forward and not let those arguments curdle into bitter and permanent feuds. Sharp and at times unpleasant debates are a necessary part of any effective political culture—but too often they take place entirely in online spaces owned by corporations that use our outrage and insecurities to keep us locked to our screens. Try whenever possible to debate your comrades in spaces where you are looking at each other and not your number of likes.

"Pessimism of the intellect, optimism of the will."

I started this book plagiarizing Marx and Engels and I'm ending it by stealing a quote from the Italian revolutionary Antonio Gramsci. Building a movement that realizes the potential of working people to run the world requires both the inspiration to believe that it's possible and the hard-headedness to understand just how difficult it will be. Try to stay out of the twin traps of lying to yourself that things aren't bleak and wallowing in self-pity as long as we still have a chance to win.

In my experience, the best way to stay on track is to keep finding reasons to laugh—at the absurdities of capitalism and at our own sometimes clumsy efforts to challenge it. When I started going to socialist events, I was surprised at all the humor amid the passion and theory. I had thought socialists would frown upon lightheartedness in a time of so much darkness. *Nobody laughs until everybody gets fed!* It turns out I had things backward. The deepest laughter comes when you're among people who are well aware of how screwed up the world is and know that there's nothing better that they can be doing with their lives than fighting like hell to change it.

Further Reading

Honestly, you have a lot of nerve coming to this page. If you went out to dinner, would you approach the chef as you were leaving and ask where else you could go for a good meal?

For real, though, I'll be thrilled if this book has sparked your curiosity to learn more about socialism, changing the world, Roscoe Conkling, and pop culture in the 1990s. Unfortunately, I tried to come up with a list of further reading suggestions, and I failed. There's simply too much good stuff out there, and the thought of creating a list that fits on one page put my stomach in a knot. I've already footnoted like a shlazillion books, movies, and podcasts on different topics, so how about you start there?

Rather than a list of what to read next, I'll offer some tips on *how* to read.

1. Find others (or one other) to read with, whenever possible.
   In our cultural imagination, a book club is a gathering in a gorgeous sunlit suburban living room where moms drink white wine and gossip under the pretense of discussing some highbrow novel that none of them have read. Frankly, that also sounds fantastic, but book clubs and study groups are an actual thing on the left, and they're a great way to both learn more from a book than you ordinarily would and occasionally make connections that can lead to practical activity. If you're afraid of not getting the reading done, you might have larger commitment issues, in which case a low-stakes book club could be a perfect first step.

2. Consider a deep dive.
   This isn't for everyone, but it can be a wonderful intellectual

experience to spend many months closely reading and taking notes on a long and dense socialist classic. Many have done this with Karl Marx's *Capital*. I did it with Hal Draper's "Marx's Theory of Revolution" series. Other possibilities include W. E. B. Du Bois's *Black Reconstruction*, Harry Braverman's *Labor and Monopoly Capital*, and any other intimidating "classic" that many lefties tell you is "essential" without giving any indication that they've read it either. It's great if you can find others to do this with, but there's also something to be said for doing it at your own pace, at a moment in your life when you have a bit more time and focus (after a breakup, perhaps, or during the mid-summer sports lull when you find yourself watching pro lacrosse).

3. Take your time.
   Do you ever feel overwhelmed by how many things you don't know anything about? Relax. One of the great things about being a socialist is that we never stop reading, debating, and learning (see book clubs and study groups). It's okay to read slowly and intermittently. You have a whole life of learning ahead of you. And if that time turns out to be shorter than you hoped, at least you didn't spend it all cooped up inside with a book!

4. Dammit, I can't help myself. Here are a few more book suggestions that I somehow didn't mention in the footnotes:

   Rosa Luxemburg's *The Mass Strike* (on the process of revolution)

   Hadas Thier's *A People's Guide to Capitalism* (on actually understanding economics)

   Howard Zinn's *A People's History of the United States* (also everything else that man wrote)

   Mike Davis's *Prisoners of the American Dream* (on how the US labor movement got to such a weak state)

Angela Davis's *Women, Race, and Class* (on what intersectionality really means)

Mariame Kaba's *We Do This 'Til We Free Us* (on what abolition really means)

Eduardo Galeano's *Upside Down* (on Latin America and neoliberalism, but also just to experience socialist writing at its most brilliant and beautiful)

Acknowledgments

This page is usually pretty boring for everybody except those hoping to see their name (shout-out to Chester Finkelstein in Huntsville, Alabama!), so we're going to play a game in which some of these acknowledgments are real, some are made up, and you have to guess which is which!

I have to start by thanking Anthony Arnove, Julie Fain, and everyone at Haymarket Books who encouraged me to write this book and then made sure I didn't completely screw it up. Special thanks to Alan Maass and Jason Farbman for the first version, and Jim Plank and John McDonald for the second. Dao X. Tran was an amazing editor for both. Thanks also to the Nobel and Pulitzer committees for your extremely kind words that we agreed to keep private. Knowing that I was "your real first choice" means more to me than any silly prize.

I am in debt to the masochists who gave me feedback on earlier drafts. For the first version, that's Brenna Schiman, Jessica Rothenberg, Larry Dwyer, Alan Maass, Amy Muldoon, and Lucy Herschel. For the second edition, that's Naiya Edwards, Miles Vender-Wilson, Zoe Lewis, Lucy Herschel, LJ Katch, Dina Gilio-Whitaker, Ragina Johnson, Brian Ward, Julian Guerrero, Alan Maass, and Amy Muldoon. The people whose names appear twice deserve combat pay and should probably learn to say no. I also want to thank Ashley Dawson, Rebecca Weston, and Melinda Maynor Lowery for answering my questions in their areas of expertise without once saying, "How are you being allowed to write a book?"

I am also grateful for the assistance, tough love, and commemorative bobblehead dolls that I received from the Wichita Center for Deep Sea Exploration, Shorty and Ray Ray from the Center for the Study of Informality, and Dalton Reed and Reed Dalton at the Institute for Applied Whiteness Studies.

My political foundation comes from literally hundreds of people who influenced me in the International Socialist Organization, as well as a number of inspiring fighters I've had the privilege to work with over the years in various movements for economic and social justice. Most recently I've learned from and laughed with my comrades in the Working-Class Heroes media collective: Yanny Guzmán, Khadija Mehter, Mel Gonzalez, Heather Ramirez, Adan Palermo, Francely Flores, Lupita Romero, and Julian Guerrero. One of the highlights of our work has been covering the story of Prakash Churaman, whose courageous fight to win his freedom inspired me and so many others.

There are so many friends and loved ones who helped me write this book by serving as sounding boards, writing buddies, or ice sculpture models. Those I haven't already mentioned include Lee Wengraf, Khury Peterson-Smith, Jen Roesch, Matt Swagler, Pranav Jani, Hadas Thier, Llana Barber, Sean Petty, and Manijeh Moradian. For allowing me to let off steam in the sparring gym, I want to thank Connor McGregor, Tyson Fury, and the late Betty White.

These pandemic years have been rough. I don't know if I could have written this revised book without my therapist. While we're at it, thank you workers of SEIU 1199 for winning contracts that cover mental health care on my wife's plan.

Lastly, of course I have to thank my family, the Italian Mafia. I can't imagine Haymarket would've agreed to this without your persuasive arguments. Also my other family: Mom, Dads, Sis, Cousins, In-Laws, and the title-less Jeff. And of course, of course, of course: Lucy, LJ, and Nadine. I dedicate this book to you. *Womp womp.*

Index

About Haymarket Books

Haymarket Books is a radical, independent, nonprofit book publisher based in Chicago. Our mission is to publish books that contribute to struggles for social and economic justice. We strive to make our books a vibrant and organic part of social movements and the education and development of a critical, engaged, and internationalist Left.

We take inspiration and courage from our namesakes, the Haymarket Martyrs, who gave their lives fighting for a better world. Their 1886 struggle for the eight-hour day—which gave us May Day, the international workers' holiday—reminds workers around the world that ordinary people can organize and struggle for their own liberation. These struggles—against oppression, exploitation, environmental devastation, and war—continue today across the globe.

Since our founding in 2001, Haymarket has published more than nine hundred titles. Radically independent, we seek to drive a wedge into the risk-averse world of corporate book publishing. Our authors include Angela Y. Davis, Arundhati Roy, Keeanga-Yamahtta Taylor, Eve Ewing, Aja Monet, Mariame Kaba, Naomi Klein, Rebecca Solnit, Olúfẹ́mi O. Táíwò, Mohammed El-Kurd, José Olivarez, Noam Chomsky, Winona LaDuke, Robyn Maynard, Leanne Betasamosake Simpson, Howard Zinn, Mike Davis, Marc Lamont Hill, Dave Zirin, Astra Taylor, and Amy Goodman, among many other leading writers of our time. We are also the trade publishers of the acclaimed Historical Materialism Book Series.

Haymarket also manages a vibrant community organizing and event space in Chicago, Haymarket House, the popular Haymarket Books Live event series and podcast, and the annual Socialism Conference.

Also Available from Haymarket Books

Abolishing State Violence: A World Beyond Bombs, Borders, and Cages
Ray Acheson

Class Struggle Unionism
Joe Burns

The Communist Manifesto: A Road Map to History's Most Important Political Document
Frederick Engels and Karl Marx, edited by Phil Gasper

The Essential Rosa Luxemburg:
Reform or Revolution *and* The Mass Strike
Rosa Luxemburg, edited by Helen Scott

Keywords for Capitalism: Power, Society, Politics
John Patrick Leary

Marx's Capital Illustrated: An Illustrated Introduction
David Smith, illustrated by Phil Evans

Remake the World: Essays, Reflections, Rebellions
Astra Taylor

A Spectre, Haunting: On the Communist Manifesto
China Miéville

State and Revolution: Fully Annotated Edition
V. I. Lenin, edited and introduced by Todd Chretien

Also by Danny Katch

America's Got Democracy: The Making of the World's Longest-Running Reality Show

Why Bad Governments Happen to Good People

About the Author

Danny Katch is a writer from Queens, New York, and a regular contributor to *Truthout*, *Jacobin*, and *The Indypendent*. His previous books include *Why Bad Governments Happen to Good People* and *America's Got Democracy! The Making of the World's Longest Running Reality Show*.